£ 11.00.

Software Engineering

Software Engineering

Marc Thorin
Chairman of IS-AUDIT

Butterworths

London Boston Durban Singapore Sydney Toronto Wellington

First published, 1985

© Butterworth & Co (Publishers) Ltd, 1985

British Library Cataloguing in Publication Data

Thorin, Marc
  Software Engineering
  1. Electronic digital computers—Programming
  I. Title
  001.64′25   QA76.6

  ISBN 0-408-01426-1

Library of Congress Cataloging in Publication Data

Thorin, Marc
  Software Engineering

  Includes index
  1. Electronic digital computers—Programming
  I. Title
  QA76.6.T474   1985   001.64′2   84-23031

  ISBN 0-408-01426-1

Photoset by Butterworths Litho Preparation Department
Printed and bound in Great Britain by Thetford Press Ltd., Thetford, Norfolk

Preface

At one time, writing software was akin to an aesthetic activity or at least some individual craftsmanship; no doubt we shall always enjoy computer games and the entertainment aspect of the computer, but the output of programs has now grown too much not to be considered as an economic activity just as serious as any other industry.

Program building is a set of the methods and rules regarding a rational output of software material. It includes the conceptual foundation, the management of the projects, the definition of criteria of quality and its appreciation, and the means and actions enabling its improvement. It concerns a wide field of application: among other activities, business management, scientific and technical computing, process control, operating systems and utility programs, aids at producing information, engineering, assisting design and teaching, and office work.

This book will introduce the user to program design and is written so that the conceptual bases as well as the main methods and rules can be readily understood. At the present time, the concepts and tools of program building are scattered over a number of publications concerning languages, programming methods, project design, files, data bases, management, scientific and industrial data processing and so on. The purpose of this book is therefore to present software engineering as a coherent and logically built synthesis, and make it possible to properly carry out an application of small or medium difficulty which can later be developed and adapted to more complex cases.

The book is divided into six chapters: Chapter 1 introduces the fundamental notions of entities, actions and programming. These are later developed in Chapters 2 and 3. Chapter 4 looks at general and technical criteria and Chapter 5 then builds on material in Chapters 2 and 3 to describe all the fundamental structures of entities. Finally, Chapter 6 uses material from Chapters 3 and 4 to expand a rational method of determining the actions.

Contents

Chapter 1

Introduction and definitions

Problem categories and specification

In general, the problems we have to solve are posed in *fuzzy terms:* there are no rules for solving them. This means that we must interpret them, make a more or less explicit expression of preferences, and use our intuition and imagination (*see Figure 1.1*). The solutions found are varied and not based on precise criteria. Most professional problems are found in this category.

Example   A stock-keeper must dispatch orders and avoid both running out of or keeping too much stock. He is also unable to plan consumption, even in statistical terms, and does not know the exact cost of a shortage or of an excess of stock. This would be classed as a fuzzy problem.

Other problems are posed in *accurate terms* but there is no well-known – or at least practically adequate – rule to solve them, so that finding a solution implies making a more or less arbitrary choice (*Figure 1.1*). It is only with hindsight that the appropriateness of the solutions or of the steps taken to reach it become apparent.

Example   A caterer must supply regular customers yet reduce fuel consumption to a minimum. He faces a clear-cut problem (if, for instance, we assume that consumption is proportional to distance), but he is more likely to trust to intuition to solve his problem and not an estimate of all the possible solutions.

Most problems in higher mathematics and many games come into this category.

Finally some problems are stated in precise terms and one or more practically adequate rules lead to a unique or acceptable solution; if used mechanically, the rules infallibly lead to solutions. These problems may be solved *automatically*. Most repetitive and simple tasks belong to this category.

Example   Writing out fiscal sheets and management charts from accounting records.

Such problems may be considered machine solvable.

Remark   A machine may also be used to make experiments easier, so long as the problem is well defined, even when there is no rule that might be applied to solve it. In this case the problem is not actually resolved, but only simulated.

The estimate does not then rely on the solution but on the solving rule(s).

Example   The builders of a lift may choose to make it work call after call, as in the case of a low block of flats. They may, however, choose to take into account all the calls simultaneously and even the moves of other lifts, such as in a high-rise block. This choice, as well as the number of lifts required, may be guided by a *simulation*.

Stating a problem to be solved is called the *specification* of the problem. Since the specification is written in natural language,

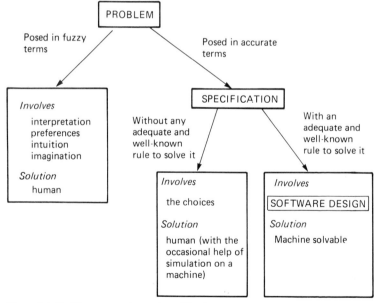

Figure 1.1 Problem categories and specification

wording proves much harder than at first appears, because the way we address each other may contain some of the following pitfalls:

- sub-specification, the omission of a detail that one, unconsciously, feels is obvious;
- ambiguity or vagueness of the terms used, that the hearer, unconsciously again, rectifies;
- contradiction or inconsistency resulting from lack of reflection;
- over-specification, addition of a detail irrelevant to the stating of the problem, but anticipating its solution.

Specification is carried out before the software design proper; but the latter cannot be effectively completed without being aware that the problems to be solved are seldom well specified.

Example   An exercise suggested for beginners in software design is often 'compute prime numbers', but in fact to test if a given number is prime or not, and to compute all the prime numbers with a range are two altogether distinct problems, each with a different solution. In the management field where problems are much harder to state correctly, insufficient specifications often cause later conflicts, if not law suits.

Algorithms, entities and actions

All the rules leading to the solution of an automatically solvable problem must describe the following *indissociable* items accurately:

- *entities* whose existence is necessary or at least useful to apply the rules,
- *actions* which will operate on the entities.

The set of rules for solving a problem is called an algorithm (*Figure 1.2*).

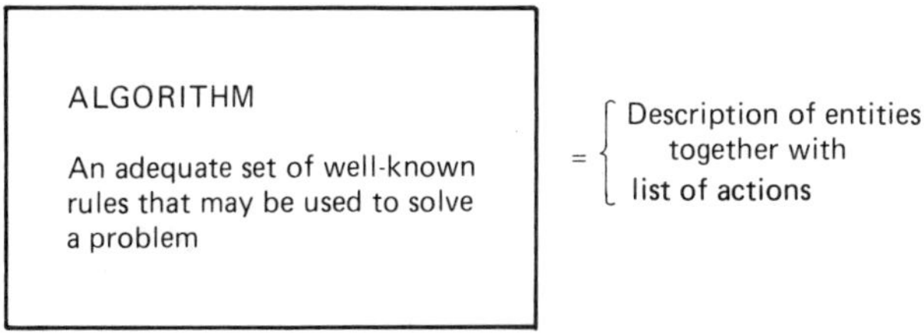

Figure 1.2 An algorithm

Example the following entities could be displayed in a schematic check-list for a dam:

- fathom,
- button controlling sluice opening,
- button controlling sluice lock.

The actions involved in operating the dam would be:

- if the level exceeds a given maximum, press the opening button;
- if the level is below a given minimum, press the lock button.

Remark The etymology of the word 'algorithm' is purely historical; it is derived from the name of a 9th century Arab mathematician.

Example An algorithm to calculate the occurrence of the frequency for each letter in a text of some length (which may be useful in cryptography) is described by the entities:

- letters from A to Z (there are 26 of them),
- special signs: blank, dot, comma, etc.,
- characters: any letter or any special sign,
- text,
- counts of each letter (there are 26),
- number of letters in the text;

and the actions:

- put all counts to zero as well as the number of letters in the text,
- read the text from the beginning to the end character after character and for each of these:

  - for a special sign, do nothing
  - for a letter, increase by 1 the count of the corresponding letter as well as the number of letters in the text and print the result.

Remark An algorithm is of practical interest only if it describes a limited number of entities and actions, and provided the latter may be carried out within a reasonable time.

The processor, sensor and effector

A prerequisite to working any algorithm automatically is the presence of a machine able to:

- take into account the entities described in the algorithm, that is, examine and/or change some of their characteristics if they exist outside the processor itself and do not depend on it, or create them if they do not already exist;
- carry out the actions planned in the algorithm.

Each part (organ) enabling us to examine some existing characteristics of an exterior entity is called a *sensor* and each part (tool) that can change these characteristics, an *effector*. One part of the machine may be both a sensor and an effector.

The *processor* is each part that is able to carry out actions. The kinds of characteristics fed directly from a sensor to a processor or from a processor to a sensor are called the *primitive types* of the processor; the actions likely to be dealt with directly by a processor are called *primitive actions* (*Figure 1.3*).

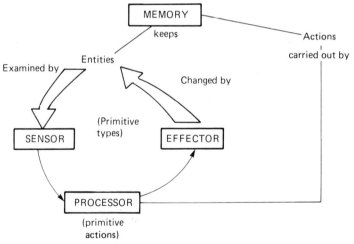

Figure 1.3 Processor, sensor, effector and memory

Remark   An effector may not necessarily be an actual tool but a line of communication or another processor.

Example   If we press the following keys on a calculator:

2 + 3 =

or, on another calculator,

2 ENTER 3 +

in each case, we apply an algorithm of addition. Each finger pressure is an entity, the keys are sensors, the device displaying the result is an effector whose only primitive type generally consists of the set of all the figures written with, say, ten decimal numbers; adding two numbers is a primitive action of the calculator processor, as is acknowledging a pressed key and displaying the result.

A machine is wholly defined by the primitive types of the entities that it can take into account through its sensors and effectors, and by the list of the primitive actions of its processors.

Although other techniques (mechanical, optical or pneumatic) may be used in sensors, effectors and processors, reasons of size, energy consumption and cost suggest the use of electronics. It naturally follows that the characteristics of the entities will eventually be received, supplied and dealt with through levels of voltage or current. Moreover the transmission and treatment (memorization in particular) of these levels proves much easier if they are reduced to a finite set of discontinuous values (even at the cost of an approximation, if they were not intrinsically so already).

Example   It is usually sufficient to know the temperature of an oven only to the nearest degree, or to be able to manipulate a tool only to the nearest hundredth of a millimetre (in common appliances). The advantage of this is that algorithms – of heating in the first case, of positioning the part in the second case – could be carried out by the same standard (albeit complex) processor, linked to different sensors and effectors.

Memory

When the description of entities and the list of actions are not extremely simple, it is more convenient to communicate them all at one time and store them in *memories* in the machine rather than supply them piecemeal.

Memories can be divided into:

- quick-access, low-capacity memory (called 'main' or 'inner' memory) storing the description of the entities and the list of the actions, frequently within a set period of time;

- high-capacity, slow-access memory (called 'outer' memory) keeping in store all the other descriptions and lists of actions and unaffected by power cuts – a permanent memory.

Example For a very few simple calculation (a few operations) a calculator without a memory is enough; for a rather complex calculation (a few operations on dozens of entities, or operations on a few entities) it is preferable to use a memory calculator with one or several memories. In the case of complex computing (hundreds of entities and/or operations) we need more than a hand calculator.

Memories allow us to set up combinations starting from primitive actions and types and progressing to new global non-primitive types and actions.

Example Suppose we set up and put into a memory a list of entities and calculations giving the square root (even of a negative number) on a programming calculator which has neither the primitive type 'complex' not the primitive action 'compute to the power one half'. We then virtually create a new machine which can deal with these functions.

Remark An inner memory reacts practically like an element of the processor, and an outer memory like a sensor and/or effector, hence their respective names.

We can now define a computer as a machine dealing with entities through the description of discontinuous characteristics, able to carry out a certain number of primitive actions, and equipped with one or more memories. A word processor or a robot are both examples of computers.

Program design

Artificial language

An algorithm is written in a natural language such as English and is first meant for a human interlocutor. Now, human language is rich and varied but often ambiguous, and much is expected from the intelligence, knowledge and imagination of the interlocutor – attributes with which no processor is endowed. Consequently it is impossible to present the latter with an algorithm in natural language; further, human senses and organs differ enormously from electronic sensors and effectors.

Example   In the algorithm of calculation of occurrence frequency for letters in a text, words and phrases like 'corresponding', 'from the beginning to the end' and 'each' must be carried out, using means and tools not available to an electronic machine.

So we have to reduce the algorithm to an equivalent description of entities and actions expressed in an *artificial language* which is bare but not ambiguous and which defines only:

- certain characteristics among a predefined set of types which may be attributed to the entities:
- the execution of simple statements (with possibly a few totally uncontroversial conditions) among a predefined set of actions.

The program

A description in artificial or *programming language* (coding language) is called a *program* (code).
The task of turning the algorithm into a program is known as *program design*, a term whose meaning clearly expresses the architectural work necessary to the building of the program from an algorithm (*Figure 1.4*).

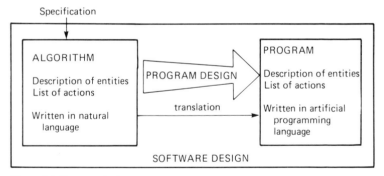

Figure 1.4 Program design

Example   Below is an algorithm for the transcription of a Roman number into an Arabic numeral; each letter stands for a precise value.

I	equals	1
V	equals	5
X	equals	10

L   equals   50
C   equals   100
D   equals   500
M   equals   1000

In a Roman number the value attributed to each letter is used to find the total value of the number. This total value depends on the order of the letters. If a letter is followed by a letter of equal or inferior value, then the values of all the letters are simply added. If, however, a letter is followed by a letter of a greater value, then the first letter is subtracted from the following letter. For example, CXI equals $100 + 10 + 1$, that is 111, and XCIX equals $-10 + 100 - 1 + 10$, that is 99. Designing such an algorithm may lead to the following program in a pseudo-programming language:

- create an entity R likely to contain letters;
- give it a series of letters standing for a Roman number;
- calculate the number of letters in R, let it be L;
- create an entity V likely to contain L components, with integer values;
- from the first component in V to the last one:
  - give it value 1 if the letter in the same row in R is 'I',
  - give it value 5 if the letter in the same row in R is 'V', . . .;
- create an entity X likely to contain an integer;
- give it the value of the last component in V;
- from the first component in V to the last but one:
  - add its value to the value X, if the value of the next component is inferior or equal,
  - otherwise subtract it;
- print the value of X.

Designing a program from an algorithm is a complex business. Descriptions and statements intended for a machine are often devoid of common sense, apart from which using any artificial language can be tedious and awkward.

Methods and rules of program design

Like any complex business, the design must be achieved in keeping with some methods and rules. Before looking closely at these, we must examine the entities and actions that are likely to be dealt with by a processor (remembering that they are interdependent) and then lay down criteria for proper design.

Example   In order to appreciate the complexity of design, we can tackle the problem of transcribing an ordinary number into Roman numerals. Here is its very simple algorithm:

- in the number given, let n be the figure in a chosen row, A the Roman letter equal to the unit in the same row, B the letter equal to five units in the same row, C the letter equal to the unit in the superior row; then:
- if $0 \leq n < 4$, it is transcribed by n times A
- if $n = 4$, by A concatenated (linked together) with B
- if $5 \leq n < 9$, by B concatenated with $(n-5)$ times A
- if $n = 9$, by A concatenated with C. The transcriptions of each figure are then linked together in the proper order.

Chapter 2
Entities

Introduction

So far we have seen that communication between the processor
and sensor or effector of an automatic electronic machine is
performed by means of discontinuous, predefined levels (of
voltage or current) in a set of countable possible values – the
nature of the set being designated by the word type.

Information and consistency domains

An entity whose every characteristic is such a value, is called
information and the *consistency domain* the set of possible values
(*Figure 2.1*).

Example   Suppose that a cheque is processed automatically by a
 bank. The amount of money on the cheque is a piece of
 information whose type is determined by say, the set of numbers
 defined to the nearest hundredth and includes all numbers
 between 5 and the balance of the account minus 0.5. Each figure
 of the amount processed automatically by a machine that drafts
 the sum in letters, is a piece of information whose types are
 defined by the digits 1 to 9 for the first figure and 0 to 9 for the
 following figures.

Atomic information

An item of *atomic information* in a given program design is an
entity which is not broken up by an action: it may be considered as
indivisible (*Figure 2.2*).

Example   In the printing of a company's payroll, a person's name
 and wages are items of atomic information, because a fragment
 from one or the other has no meaning by itself. In a search for

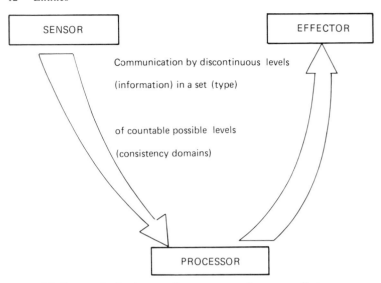

Figure 2.1 Communication between the processor and sensor or effector

double consonants in a text, the atomic information is a cut-off letter or sign.

So an actual – and consistent – item of atomic information is defined as a *non-dissociable triplet* consisting of:

- its *value* (the level achieved at a given time among all possible levels);
- its *type* (the set of countable possible levels, some of which may be equipped with operations);
- its *name* or identifier (so that it may be referred to whatever its value may be, in the design and the program).

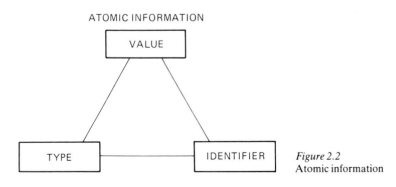

Figure 2.2
Atomic information

Remark   Primitive languages (machine languages) were only able to describe the values and their location (which particular sensor or effector or memory cell). Early on, the need to label entities with identifiers was recognized, except for those entities which do not change value (constants) and those whose values are given by their representations (then called literal constants). Later the notion of type, which characterizes a set (with the operations defined on the elements in it), was acknowledged.

Example   A person's temperature may be measured periodically and defined within the set of values from 35.0 to 42.0 °C in steps of 0.1 °C. This is the set of countable levels – the type. The value 37.0 °C is the actualization of a level; it may be called 'normal temperature', but as it is a constant, it need not be given a name. Only the comparison between two temperatures is defined and the processor is expected to be programmed to refuse an aberrant action such as adding two temperatures, dividing a temperature by an integer or taking into account an excessively high or low value.

The same entity can have several values coming one after another as a result of outside influences or actions from the processor. It is then usually considered to be a single entity of variable value not identified by its name.

Example   Successive measures that are dealt with individually are referred to by a single name. Similarly, a final result calculated by accumulating intermediary results would also be referred to by a single name.

Rarely does the same entity change its name or its type.

Example   Two programs, written by two different people and then integrated into one, can name the same entity using different identifiers; a certain number of temperatures which have already been measured may entail calculating the average (whereas initially, adding the temperatures and dividing them by an integer was excluded).

Main types of information

The *main types* of information are:

- the *numerical* type – finite subsets of integers, fractions, or complex or imaginary numbers;
- the *character string* type – finite series of letters, digits or other signs;

- the *logical* type – set of the two 'true' and 'false' elements;
- the *enumeration* type – set of any values given in a list.

The names given to items of information are given freely (except for a few syntactic purely technical constraints).

The possible values are derived from the types and represented in a design or program in a similar way to that of everyday writing.

Time and event

One item of atomic information that is often essential is the measurement of *time*, given by a special sensor (a clock) as either a number or a digit string. The clock is an effector when initialized, that is, set at the right time.

Another important item of atomic information is the occurrence of an *event*, often comparable to a logical variable that changes value whenever an outside entity has just been created, destroyed or given a certain characteristic. The timer is a clock that works backwards and is used as an effector when initialized to a given time lag, and works as a sensor at the end of the time lag, when triggering an event.

Example   An alarm system working by detection of an event (such as the interruption of a light beam), deals with the event by initializing a timer. If no de-activating event occurs, it will trigger a signal at the end of the time lag.

Compound information, fields and groups

It is very often necessary to deal globally with a group of several types of atomic informations.

Example   A customer's invoice may be characterized by his name, address and terms of payment.

Such a *group* of information is called *compound information*, and each item of the atomic information, a *field* (*Figure 2.3*). A field may itself be a group.

Example   A person's address is the group of street number, road name, town name and postal code.
Groups may be:

- *Invariable* when the types and numbers of the fields do not vary (*Figure 2.4*).

COMPOUND INFORMATION
(group)

Atomic information   Atomic information
(field)   (field)
- - -

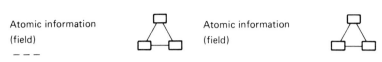

Figure 2.3 Compound information

Invariable

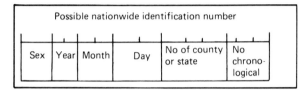

Possible nationwide identification number					
Sex	Year	Month	Day	No of county or state	No chrono-logical

Variable through iteration

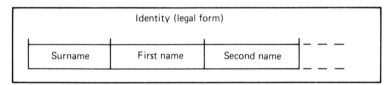

Identity (legal form)			
Surname	First name	Second name	- - -

Variable through recursion

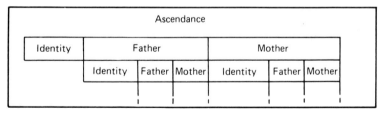

Variant

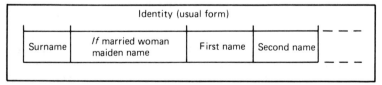

Figure 2.4 Examples of compound information

Example The nationwide identification of a person might consist of fields that are, always identical with values only varying from one individual to another one. In the same way, the measurement of temperature and time is an invariable group of two variable fields.

- *Variable through iteration*, that is, the repetition – an indeterminate number of times – of one or several fields of invariable type (*Figure 2.4*).

Example The group first name, possibly second or further names and surname consists of a variable number of fields, of which there are at least two.

- *Variable through recursion*, that is, the subdivision of one or several fields of invariable type into elements including a field of the same type (*Figure 2.4*).

Example A person described by his parents identity, father and mother, the latter parents being described by their respective parents identities, and so on.

- *Variant*, when the fields are of variable type and number (*Figure 2.4*).

Example A man's name usually includes a single surname, but a married woman's also includes another field (her maiden name), besides a number – variable through iteration – of given names.

Data collection

Data that are linked together in some way by nature or by function relations are often gathered into collections. A collection is several items of information partly or entirely dealt with by given algorithms.

Records

A *record* is either atomic or compound information which belongs to a collection (*Figure 2.5*).

Example In the case of the management of orders of stock in a company, the record would consist of the group characterizing the product (Quantity, unit price, number in the catalogue, and so on); the atomic information would be the date and is included

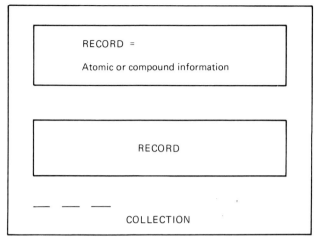

Figure 2.5 A record

in the record. Both the record and atomic information are usually dealt with together. The order list is the collection of these records.

Files

A collection made up only of records of the same nature is called a *file* (*Figure 2.6*).

Example   The collection of all the products described by (compound) information of a given kind, even when its groups are variable or variant, is the products' file.

All the records in a file, being of the same nature, can be considered as the different *instantiations* (concrete instances) of a single entity, in which only the values vary (apart from a few exceptions).

Example   The file of all the car products manufactured and ready for delivery may be considered as a collection of all the actual instantiations at a given moment of the car entity.

It is therefore impossible for an algorithm to refer to one of several precise instantiations in a collection by the identifier. Calling each one by a different name would cancel any benefit gained by gathering them into a collection; furthermore, it would not be feasible because of their number.

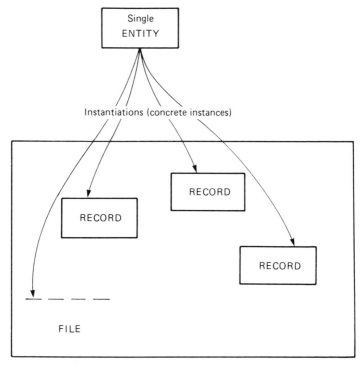

Figure 2.6 A file

It is however possible and feasible, and sometimes necessary, to keep a field of each record for a number or a designation which characterizes it: such a field is not a name for the algorithm, but a value.

Example   A car manufacturer may refer to each of several models as a different entity with a name of its own. In each model, a new car produced is an instantiation without any specific name. Some fields, however, have specific values (frame number, engine number), yet those values need not play a more particular role than values common to other instantiations (colour, date of the making).

Data base

A collection built up of differing kinds of records which correspond to one another through some atomic or compound information in one or several algorithms is called a *data base* (*Figure 2.7*).

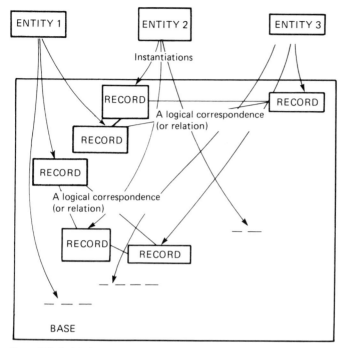

Figure 2.7 A data base

Example   A collection of orders, of products available in stock, of products in the making and of all the products in the catalogue, all contain partly redundant descriptions of the products. These collections can be gathered into a base where there is a single description of every product.

The correspondence between records is associated with one or more algorithms and is not a feature of the collection. We often speak of 'logical correspondence' or 'logical relation' in order to emphasize the difference between this correspondence and that of the layout of the entities in a memory.

Example   In the preceding base, the goods that are listed in the catalogue but not in the make nor in stock, do not concern an accountancy algorithm, which consequently will not set up any correspondence between them.

Remark   A file is, in fact, only a particularly simple data base; and a data base where different kinds of records have no connection with each other, is nothing but a mixture of files.

A data base – usually a voluminous collection dealt with by varied programs – exists permanently even though it may constantly be partly altered. A file, however, may not exist at a particular time, for example, as in a collection of measurements that are periodically sent by a device, processed at once and then discarded.

Organization and access

Two basic, interdependent aspects of a collection need consideration:

- the description of the whole of the collection: that is the problem of *organization*;
- the method of accessing one or more individual records: that is, the problem of *access*.

Organization and access are notions related to an algorithm, and are not unique features of a collection. For any given collection we may very often find at least several interesting ways of organizing and accessing the records (*Figures 2.8* and *2.9*); further, the very notion of a record in a collection is itself related to an algorithm. We may emphasize this abstract quality by calling it 'conceptual organization', or 'logical organization', and 'logical access', so as to make a clear distinction between the physical layout of items in the memories and the operations carried out there.

Example A printer receives a dictionary as an uninterrupted stream of typed characters. The binder sees it as a set of numbered sections to be bound together. The reader sees it differently again, as an alphabetically ordered set of indexes (the few letters printed on the top corners of the pages) which first enables him to find the right page, then, as a list of words on a page. The uses of the same medium (printed papers) are so different that the errors (in printing, binding, reading) have nothing in common.

The access may be meant to:

- *create* and initialize the value of a record (simultaneously since a record, the instantiation of an entity, cannot exist without possessing some value);
- *update* the value;

- *enquire about its existence* (The answer 'true' or 'false' applying to the question: 'Is there such a record of such a value?');
- *enquire about the value* (by asking 'What are the values of the fields of a record with such characteristics?'), which is a function;
- *cancel* the existence and the value of a record.

Creating, updating and cancelling are *primitives of access*.

The collection

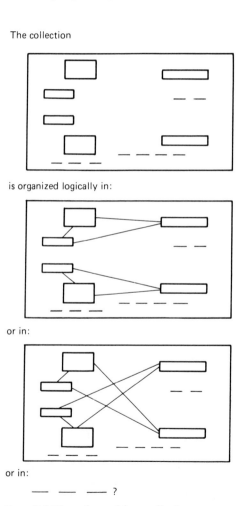

is organized logically in:

or in:

or in:

Figure 2.8 Ways of organizing a collection

The access

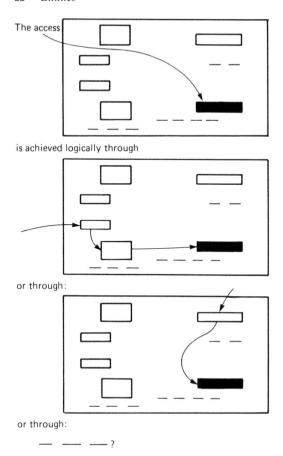

is achieved logically through

or through:

or through:

— —— —— ?

Figure 2.9 Ways of accessing records

Organization of a file

We have seen that a file is a collection of records of the same kind. When there is no logical correspondence between the records of a file, logical organization of the file does not exist and so the file need not be described (except through the nature of its records). This is known as an unorganized *heap* in the considered algorithm.

Example   We can say that the heap of record cards of patients examined by a doctor in one day is not organized, except through the chronological order of the examinations; this may be of no interest for any algorithm whatsoever.

Conversely there are as many genuine logical organizations as interesting ways of setting up logical correspondences between records.

Example   One convenient way of organizing a doctor's card's is in alphabetical order of his patients' names. Another way of special interest for some hereditary diseases – is to link each patient's card with his or her parents', brothers' and sisters' (if they are the same doctor's patients). If the file is classified in alphabetical order, the relation 'be a relative' is materialized by cross references and not a juxtaposition of cards, since the mother sometimes bears a different name and fathers and sons children are sometimes laid apart because of homonyms. If the file were to use the alphabetical order of surnames only, then the relationships of the individuals are not apparent.

Consequently, an algorithm has to describe every logical organization of the collection it uses. In its most general form, the conceptual organization of a file connects a characteristic of the record to each of the records that is logically related to it; on a paper where the whole file would be printed, this would amount to tracing links between them.

More particularly, the relations are seldom symmetrical, and the logical organization may be represented by an *oriented graph* (*Figure 2.10*): each record is accompanied only by the fields

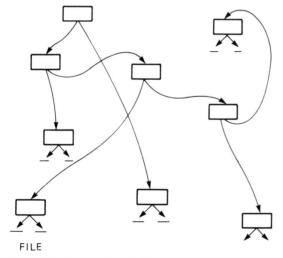

FILE

Figure 2.10 Organization of a file

characterizing records logically following in the relation (which would amount, on the same paper, to tracing arrows and not simply links); such records are called its *direct descendants*. The descendants of direct descendants are not qualified by an adjective; sometimes a record happens to be its own descendant.

Very often each record has only one direct descendant (except the last one, of course). The oriented graph is then named a *chain*, and each direct descendant, a *follower*.

Example   The file of the employees in a company may be organized according to the alphabetical order of their full names (a chain), to the chronological order of enrolment (another chain), to their position in the management hierarchy (a head clerk will have only direct descendants, unlike the head of a department), to their functions (for instance in the flow of information concerning purchases).

A record is called *ascendant* of its descendants in a graph, and *precedent* of its follower in a chain.

Each field intended to refer to related records can:

- either represent a value specific to one or several appointed records; this field serves only to access and not to any other part of the algorithm. Such a field is known as a *pointer*.
- or be a field value of one or several records serving to elucidate the algorithm, and not necessarily limited only to access. In this case, the field is called a *key* (*Figure 2.11*).

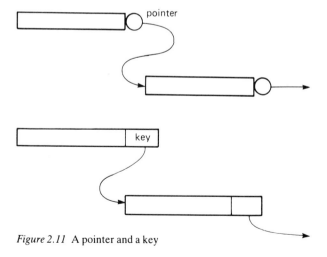

Figure 2.11 A pointer and a key

The fields linked to a record may combine pointers and keys but one or several pointers rarely happen to be mixed with one or several keys, since access is then more complicated. The same work 'key' is also kept for the field values that refer to the record, following a simple calculation.

Example   In a file of employees, the operation of pointing out the next name in a list in alphabetrical order is a pointer and serves to access only; it is not able to compute wages. Conversely, a hierarchical coefficient is a key relating all the equals and may be used to compute the amount of a bonus specific of a level.

Examples of a pointer and key are shown in *Figures 2.12* and *2.13*.

Access in a file

In a file, the logical access to a record can first be achieved with the aid of an indicated *value* (as all the records are the same kind, neither the type of information nor the name of a field, or the names of several fields, are different; it is therefore significant to access any particular record). The access to a record can be defined as follows:

- if the given value of a field (or the given values of several fields) characterizes one single record, the access is said to be *absolute* (*Figure 2.14*);
- if the value of the field should occur an indefinite number of times, the access is called *associative* (*Figure 2.15*).

Example   In a file of patients, full names serve only as keys for an absolute access; the retrieval of the names of, say, the over-65s, smokers, and patients whose last visit to the doctor dates back over a year, is an associative access.

Moreover the access to a record in a genuinely organized file (and not in a heap) can be carried out through the retrieval of descendants (or of the only follower in the case of a chain); this access is called *relative*. More precisely, if, for each inquiry, only one of the descendants – perhaps the only one – at most is kept, the access is qualified as *iterative* (*Figure 2.16*). If several descendants happen to be kept, the inquiry taking place simultaneously for each of them, the access is said to be *recursive* (*Figure 2.17*).

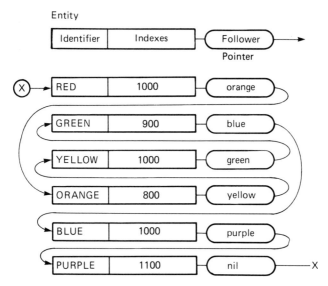

Figure 2.12 Example of a pointer.

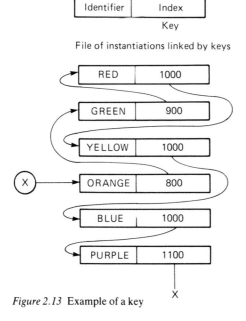

Figure 2.13 Example of a key

Entity

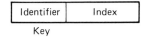

Key

Absolute access on the 'identifier' key (no homonymy)

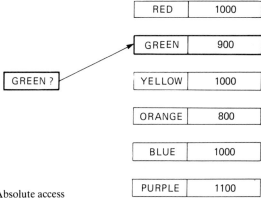

Figure 2.14 Absolute access

Entity

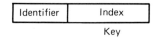

Key

Associative access on the 'index' key (possible homonymy)

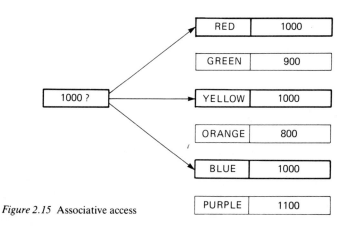

Figure 2.15 Associative access

Entity

Iterative relative access

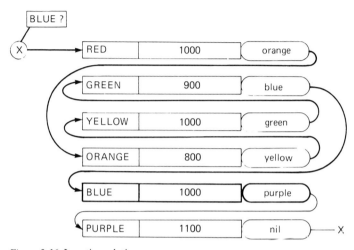

Figure 2.16 Iterative relative access

Example   Monthly payrolls are practically always worked out from the file of the employees organized in a chain in alphabetical order with an iterative relative access; the list of a director's subordinates is set up through recursive relative access to sub-directors, then to heads of departments, then to head clerks and lastly to employees, namely to the subordinates' subordinates, and so on.

These modes of access may be combined but are seldom in a file.

Example   The logical access to a patient's two parents is relative and iterative for the doctor who needs the two cards; for the secretary who tries to actually find them in an disorganized heap, the two accesses are absolute – carried out by searching cards until the two right ones are found – or, alternatively, associative – when the cards have notches and are selected by a rail device.

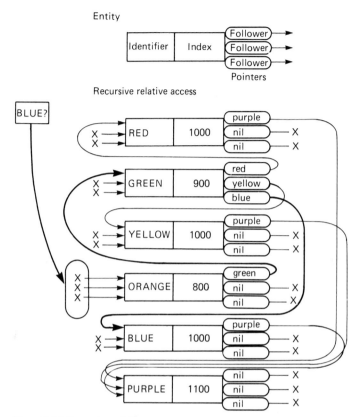

Figure 2.17 Recursive relative access

Remark   Access by key is not really different from access by value (absolute when iterative, associative when recursive), as it is based on the value of a field.

Organization of a data base in a network of plex structure

A data base is characterized by the logical relations existing between records: consequently it cannot be reduced to an disorganized heap.

Like a file, a data base may be logically organized as a graph. The base is never reduced to a chain because a single follower relation between records of different kinds is too primitive to be of practical interest. Organization as a graph is then called a *network* or a *plex* (*Figure 2.18*).

Entities

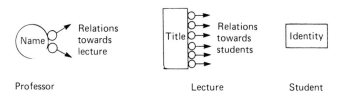

Professor   Lecture   Student

University : base organized in a network, navigation

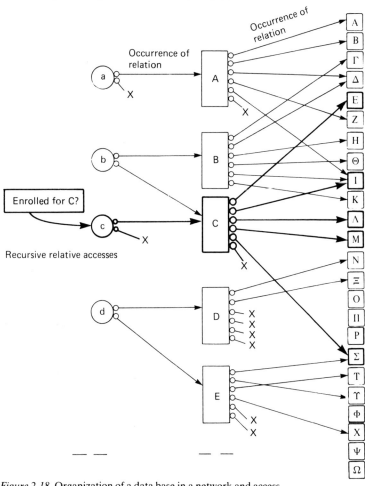

Figure 2.18 Organization of a data base in a network and access

Example   The academic staff of a college (its professors and lecturers) and its students may be described in such a network. Each professor has the lectures he gives for descendants and each lecture has the students enrolled for it for descendants. No student has any descendant but is himself a direct descendant of one or several lectures and thus an indirect descendant of the professors. When a lecture is given by several cooperating professors, it has several ascendants.

In a network base, we try to reduce the redundancy of information by keeping only the minimum in each record. Consequently, data relations are represented more easily by pointers than by keys.

Example   For each of the 'lecture' records, it is simpler to associate a pointer with each student enrolled rather than a key, (for instance, his full name).

The use of the word 'network' or 'plex' – as distinct from that of 'graph' for a file – is adequate because the relations in a data base are considered to be between the entities themselves, rather than between instantiated records (called instantiations of relation).

Example   The relation between the general professor 'entity' and the general lecture 'entity' is not the instantiation of the relation: professor Y gives lecture Z.

A frequent and particular case of a network is when each entity or record is a non-single descendant of one and only one other, (except the first); the graph is then called a *tree* and the organization qualified as *hierarchical*.

Example   A complex machine may be described by a list of its parts; the parts by a list of the sub-parts, and so on down to the last elements. But the college in the preceding example cannot be organized hierarchically: if it were, then each lecture would be given by only one lecturer and each student would be enrolled for only one lecture.

When a record is a descendant of a small number of records, the base may be represented by several coexisting but disconnected hierarchical organizations, multiple descendants being copied ones in each of these.

Example   When a lecture is given by only one professor and when a student attends only two or three lectures, it may prove practicable to organize the preceding base as a hierarchy of each professor in relation to his lectures, and of each lecture in relation to his students, the students appearing in as many hierarchies as lectures they attend.

Access in a network or plex data base

In a data base organized as a network we might assume access to be by value to a record. Such a method of organization, however, is of no help in retrieval. On the other hand, there is a disadvantage with regard to organization into several distinct files since, instead of limiting the search to the records of a same kind, we must extend it to all the records in the base.

Example   To find out the characteristics of a chosen student in the preceding data base, the organization by descendance from professors and from lectures is rather a drawback.

That is why the access by value is never used entirely by itself in a network data base: the main access is always relative – iterative or recursive – and bears the specific name of *navigation*, which suggests successive retrieval steps (each step may be locally followed by an access by value) (*Figure 2.18*).

Example   Knowing that a student attends a particular lecture given by a particular professor, we can access from the professor to his descendants (namely his lectures), then from the selected lecture to its own descendants (that is, the students enrolled for it), and ultimately we find the required record (which, for instance, enables us to trace the other lectures he has enrolled for).

Relational organizations of a data base

A base can also be organized into logical files ('logical' emphasizing the difference from the possible physical layout), each file corresponding to a type of record. In other words each logical file is the set of all records of the same kind. A base following such an organization is called *relational* because the records in different files have to be related in some way (*Figure 2.19*).

University : relational data base, assertion

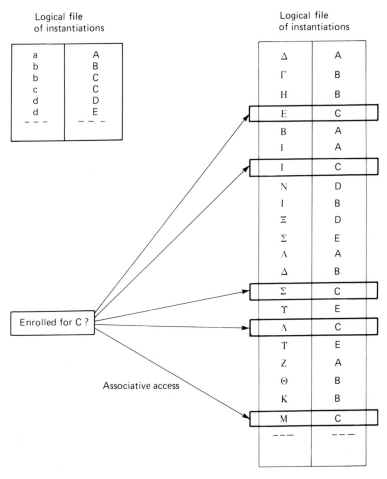

Figure 2.19 Relational organization of a data base and access

Example   A college may be represented by the logical file of the professors and the lecture(s) they give and by that of the students and the lecture(s) they attend.

In a relational data base, we try to keep the full content of each record, the relations are thus more naturally represented by keys than by pointers.

Example   In the preceding base, it is more natural to represent the relation between a professor and his students by the presence of the same lecture title in the record of the 'professors and their lectures' logical file on the one hand, and in the record of the 'students and their lectures' logical file on the other hand.

Access in a relational data base

In a relational data base, although a relative access by navigation is conceivable, the relational organization would be of no more interest than a network.

Example   When we want to make an inquiry in the preceding base, through access via a professor to his lectures, then via the latter to his students, the relational organization is rather a nuisance.

That is why relative access, as described here, is not used in a relational base. However, the main (absolute or associative) access by value is interesting, because it characterizes the required entities and not the process enabling us to reach them.

Example   An access by value to the logical file of the students and their lectures produces the record with its characteristics (for instance, all the lectures attended, even if the professors' names are not known).

The organization in logical files limits the access exclusively to records of a certain type. This type, in its turn, may be considered as an entity whose instantiations, put together, build up the content of the logical file.
   In addition, in a relational base, access by value simply extends into access by a given range of values and/or access consisting of a combination of values, and even access by subtype (that is, a subset of the logical file).

Example   In a logical file of students and their lectures, if each record includes full name, date of birth and former diploma lectures attended, then access to all the students born after a chosen date is by range of values; access to those with a particular diploma and attending a specific lecture is combined; access to those attending a lecture is an extract from a subset, as natural as the access to a single record.

When an access involves the values it is called *assertional* (*Figure 2.19*) and when the aspect of type and subtype is privileged, the access is known as *set-like*.

Remark   Another way of organizing a base may be to attribute fields to each relation (and no longer to one or the other record that it links together). This organization is called *entity relation*.

Example   In a hospital, the patients may be records whose fields are identity, registration number and file number and the doctors, records whose fields are identity and specialization; a visit or an examination is a relation to which the fields date and prescription number may be added.

In a relational organization, there would have been three logical files: the patients' (with identity, registration number and file number for each of them), the doctors' (with identities and specialities) and the visits or examinations (with patient's identity, doctor's identity, date and prescription number for each).

In a network organization, three types of records would have been dealt with: patient, doctor, visit or examimation, each patient record and doctor record being supplied with a pointer towards each of the visits or examinations (so, in order to access the doctors consulted by a given patient, it would be necessary to search for all the visits which have been paid to the doctors, then go back from these to the doctors).

Lastly, in a hierarchical organization, we would have had to state either that a doctor consulted is a descendant of a patient or the other way round, and link the examination to the doctor or the visit to the patient. For instance, it would be impossible to link a patient and his visits directly to a doctor because the relation between a patient and an examination would not be expressed – even indirectly.

This complex organization is not widespread. The network base organizations and the relational ones amount to the same, in so far as one may be translated into the other one (schema translation); but the relations between records are explicit in a network base and implicit in a relational one.

In a base, the consistency domains of items of information may not be independent; they are called *consistency constraints*.

Other entities

Our discussion so far has enabled us to reduce the description of organizations and accesses to a few general types; it should also be clear that the natures of both are abstract and have no fixed correspondences with any particular physical layout.

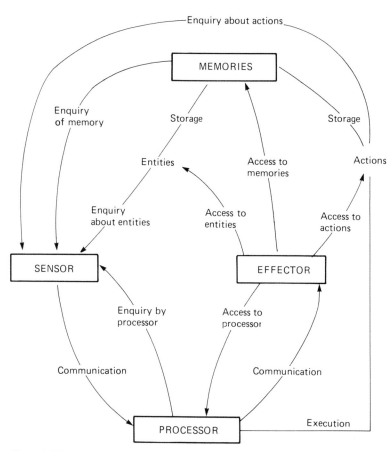

Figure 2.20 Other entities

Example The same museum may be visited systematically in several ways: by following a guidebook or an arrowed route, so as to vary and increase aesthetic emotion, or from the first to the last room on each floor retracing one's steps as little as possible, or by chronological order of exhibits. Each time the organization and access are different, illustrating their abstract nature.

The sensors and effectors, the processor itself, a whole file or a base considered as a whole must occasionally be dealt with by an algorithm as entities on which some operations (such as turning to a particular state, reservation) are performed (*Figure 2.20*).

Example A measuring device such as a voltmeter has to be calibrated (for zero position, sensitivity, range); a controlled tool such as a mechanical arm must at certain times be devoted to a given program so as to avoid aberrant moves.

It may be convenient to include the whole of a program, without any modifications, within another program. In this case, the included program would be an entity.

Example A mathematical function such as a sine.

Chapter 3

Actions

Executable, non-executable, access and interrogative statements

So far we have seen that actions performed by the processor tackled entities and were worked out through a *programming design* leading from an *algorithm* to a *program* or *code* (*Figure 3.1*).

A processor can take into account only imperative, occasionally adverbial, *statements* written in an artificial language. The statements that actually manipulate the entities are mostly called *executable statements*; those describing a type of entities, a specific entity or a collection are mostly called *non-executable statements* because no actual manipulation is implied in them. Those access statements one or several entities are usually known as *access statements* if the access is relative and query (or *interrogative statements*) if the access is provided by means of a value.

Example In a file of students and marks, the common phrase 'give such and such a student such and such a mark' corresponds to an executable statement in the program; the description 'consider the student entity as constituted of a maximal twenty alphabetical letter identity and of three marks varying from A to E' corresponds to a non-executable statement. The access 'find the next one, if any, in marks are above C' is a query. This terminology is rather vague: 'give such and such a student such and such a mark' presupposes a previous access; 'give each student E', which is a security initialization for the missing ones, may be conceived as either an actual order (executable statement) or a description (non-executable statement).

Elementary statements

As the purpose of statements is to deal with entities, the artificial language used must enable us to describe them. More precisely:

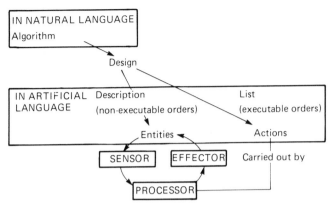

Figure 3.1 Algorithms, entities and actions

- for data items: to create them, give them values, identifiers and types;
- for data aggregates: to describe field groups;
- for data collections, to define records, organization and access.

High-level artificial language (as opposed to machine languages) are derived from American English. Obviously, artificial languages could be utterly different if they were based on a non Indo-European language.

The terminology adopted in the following passage is used in standard grammar books, and is more widely spread than the nomenclature of more modern definitions; it is thus sufficient for our purpose.

An *elementary statement* is the translation from natural language into artificial language of a sentence with only one verb (*Figure 3.2*).

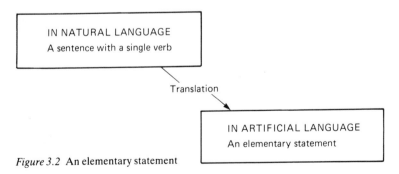

Figure 3.2 An elementary statement

Structure of a statement

Whenever it expresses a *manipulation* or a *description* of an entity, that very may be either an active infinitive (a widely spread solution avoiding any conjugation), or a verb in the imperative mood.

Two general patterns can be used to express such an elementary statement:

- verb + object + preposition + complement,
- verb + indirect object + direct object (*Figure 3.3*).

The order of the elements may be reversed when the indirect object is longer than the direct object.

The first pattern may be reduced to:

- verb (with object implied)
  Example   Stop (the execution of the program)

- verb + object

  Example   Read data X

- verb + preposition + complement

  Example   Wait until event S

but it may also be complete:

Example   Read data Y from file F

The second pattern is always complete.

Example   Give data X value V

However, when there is no risk of ambiguity, the verb may be suppressed in both patterns so as to lighten the statements: such verbs as 'do', 'give', 'compute' are generally omitted. For the same reason all the articles are dropped.

Example   'Give X the integer type' will be shortened into, let us say, 'X integer' most of the time.

Vocabulary

In the artificial language, the *vocabulary* used for these elementary statements includes:

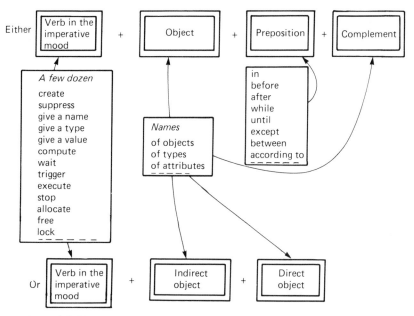

Figure 3.3 Elementary statement of manipulation or description of an entity

- verbs (a few dozen) applying to
  - data or data collections (create, suppress, build up the groups, give a value, give a name, give a type, receive or read, send or write, compute, forbid access);
  - in particular, time (wait) and events (wait, trigger);
  - programs (execute, stop execution);
  - sensors, effectors and the processor itself (allocate, free, lock. read in such a format, write in such a format);
- complements denoting
  - specific predefined objects (standard reader, keyboard, display, printer, etc.)
  - predefined types or attributes (numeric type, logical type, reading or writing formats, etc.);
- prepositions or prepositional phrases (to, from, in, before, after, while, until, with, without, except, between, according to).

Remark Most complements are data whose identifiers were chosen with hardly any restrictions.

The verb 'compute' (or 'evaluate') relates to an object generally written in a mathematical formula, with more or less powerful and numerous operators: scalar or array operators; logical operators; relational ones (operating on comparisons); linking together, slicing and set operators (union, intersection, subset selection, projection, etc.); sorting operators and so on.

When it expresses *access* to an entity, an elementary statement can in all cases be conveyed by a question with the following structure (*Figure 3.4*).

- interrogative pronoun or adjective or adverb (or phrase) introducing a clause in the indicative mood.

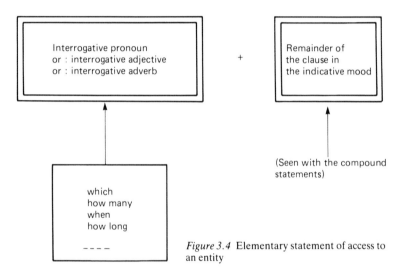

Figure 3.4 Elementary statement of access to an entity

Remark A noun clause does not vary significantly from a question because it depends on a very simple main clause (find——, is there an entity——) which can always be implied and generally is in artificial languages.

Example 'Find in file F which is the following data X' will be written as:

Which is the following X in F?

or even as:

Following X in F (the question mark being dropped).

- When the entity to be found does not belong to a collection, its identifier is used to find its value. The noun clause is then usually written as the identifier only and becomes a manipulation at the same time.

Example 'X + . . .' means 'find the value of entity X and add it to . . .'.

- The difference between a simple relative access or even an absolute access by value and an elementary manipulating statement is seldom put into words in an artificial language: the manipulating verbs 'read' and 'write' are used for both access and manipulation.

Example 'Write X + 1 in F' is an elementary statement to be found in many languages and means accede to X, add 1 to its value, accede to the next record in F, write the value found. The different notions are mixed, but the practical advantage is clear.

So the vocabulary used for these elementary statements in an artificial language includes:

- the neuter interrogative pronouns: what, which, which one, of which, to which;
- the interrogative adjective: which;
- the interrogative adverbs expressing quantity (how many, how much) and time (when, how long).

We shall look at the rest of the noun clause later as its form is close to that of compound manipulating statements.

Compound statements

The orders given to a processor are necessarily imperative and positive.

Example A statement can never be accompanied by 'occasionally' or be negative as in 'do not compute'.

Remark Most artificial languages, however, possess a null statement which expressly mentions that there is nothing to do.

Yet statements may happen not to be absolute but linked with adverbial clauses. Such statements are called *compound statements* or *compound orders* (*Figure 3.5*).

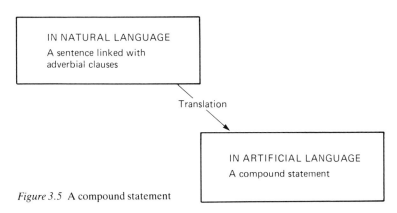

Figure 3.5 A compound statement

Example   Compute the square root of X only if X is not negative.

An adverbial manipulation statement can be expressed by relating the elementary statement to an adverbial clause introduced by a conjunction, or conjunctional phrase, of subordination containing only one condition, namely of a logical value (which may be true or false) (*Figure 3.6*). Only this structure is kept in an artificial language, although there are other possibilities in natural language.

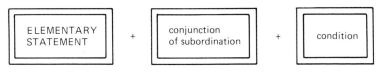

Figure 3.6 A compound order of manipulation or description of entities

The place of the adverbial clause (before or after the elementary statement) is not significant.

Example   'Read data X from file F so long as F not empty' may be expressed in ordinary language as:
'When F is not empty, read X from F and do it again.'

Similarly a question can always be expressed by the following structures:

- interrogative pronoun + 'be' conjugated + 'such as' + condition, or

Either:

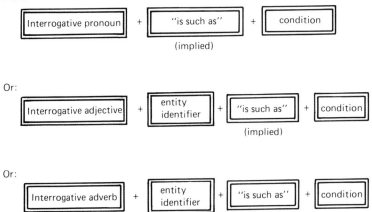

Figure 3.7 A compound order of access to an entity

- interrogative adjective + entity identifier + 'be' conjugated + 'such as' + condition, or
- interrogative adverb + entity identifier + 'be' conjugated + 'such as' + condition

or either of these forms in the plural.

For practical reasons 'be' conjugated, + 'such as' is generally omitted. So only the formulation of the condition is of any interest, and is the same as the formulation found in adverbial manipulating statements.

The condition is easily described by a logical expression with logical, relational or set operators applying to data (*Figure 3.7*).

Example   In a file, the question 'find the names of all patients over 65 who smoke' may be asked as:
'Which X in F (are such as) age >65 and smoker = yes' or
'Extract from F (age >65) and smoker'.

Procedural and non-procedural languages

When the language favours access through condition, and consequently the description of the result expected rather than the way to reach it, it is called *non-procedural*; a language which favours manipulation is typified as *procedural*.

Example In the preceding example, the two forms are non-procedural; in a procedural language, the question would be expressed as:
Read X from F if F not empty
Give up search if F empty
Print X if X's age >65 and X smoker
Do it again

Remark Non-procedural languages are closer to natural languages and the programs written in them may be roughly understood by anyone. They are more closely related to mathematical language than procedural languages, which are more analytical in form and nearer to the way machines actually do the work. For these reasons the former are often preferred by managers and mathematicians, the latter by other scientific people.

In plain procedural language, deprived of any question, all the retrieval algorithms must be written out.

Vocabulary

The conjunction or conjunctival phase can convey a plain logical condition (*Figure 3.8*).

- if . . . (or: provided, provided that, in the case when);
- except if . . . (or: unless), more simply expressed with 'if' and a condition of opposite value;
- while . . .
- until . . .

Adding link words is not indispensable but very convenient:

- according to whether . . . or . . . or (or: if . . . or . . . or);
- else . . . (otherwise . . . or else . . .).

The conjunction or conjunctival phrase can also introduce a time clause (*Figure 3.8*) expressing:

- simultaneity of a moment (when, at the time when);
- simultaneity of a lapse (as long as, in the same time as);
- repetition (whenever, each time);
- anteriority of a moment (as soon as, as early as, from the moment when);
- anteriority of a lapse (after, since);
- posteriority of a moment (until the moment when);
- posteriority of a lapse (before, pending the time when).

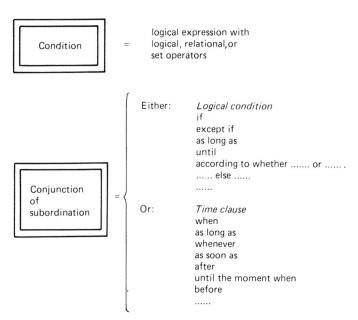

Figure 3.8 A compound order: condition, conjunction of subordination

Remark These conjunctions have rather vague meaning in natural language; their respective senses must be precisely determined in artificial language.

In an order to a processor there is no need for conjunctions expressing cause, result, purpose or concession.

Pronouns, adjectives and adverbs are either impossible (now, not only . . . but also . . ., meanwhile, etc.) or dispensable (any, both, several, all, no . . ., each, every . . ., etc.) in an artificial language. Cardinal numbers may be expressed by digits. Some elements in the language (in particular, many adverbs) are far from having a well-defined simple function and are consequently excluded.

Statements' collections

Simple or compound statements are co-ordinated (linked together) by implied 'and', which is often replaced by a special sign meaning that whenever a statement has been executed the next one must be dealt with.

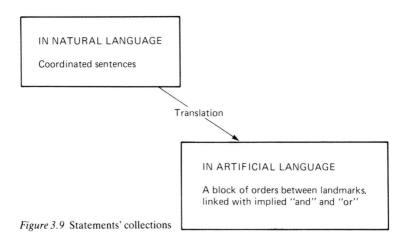

Figure 3.9 Statements' collections

Statements cannot be coordinated by 'neither . . . nor . . .' since they are positive.

We have seen that statements are conveniently coordinated by 'or' (generally implied), so as to lighten and clarify the expression of exclusive clauses (*Figure 3.9*).

Example   Compute X% discount if amount over X; or
Compute Y% discount if amount over Y, otherwise nothing.

Remark   There is no need for the other co-ordinating conjunctions in an artificial language because they express opposition, concession, restriction, cause, consequence, extra explanation or gradation (for example, 'on the contrary', 'on the other hand', 'besides', 'moreover', etc.)

The two statements 'compute' and 'assign result to' are so often linked together that they are always grouped with a special sign.

Blocks

A statements' collection that is self-sufficient is called *a block* (*Figure 3.10*).

Example   It is the proper denomination for several statements which must be linked if a condition is true: reiterating the condition for each of them would be very awkward, and skipping their execution if and only if the condition is false would be confusing.

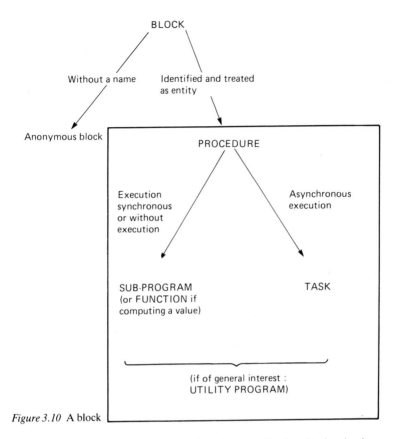

Figure 3.10 A block

A block is limited by two landmarks mentioning its beginning and its end.

Remark   Whereas it is hard to make out the elementary or compound nature of a statement, the 'block' notion is all the easier to determine since it corresponds to the usual division into chapters, paragraphs and sentences.

Procedures, tasks, sub-programs and functions

If a block may be considered as an entity by another program, which implies giving it a name, it is called a *procedure*. More accurately, a procedure is known as a *task* if it is performed simultaneously with another program, otherwise it is a *sub-program* , which may, in turn, be known as a *function* if its only purpose is to return a value. A task or sub-program intended for miscellaneous applications is more often called a utility.

An artificial language may thus include landmarks limiting a procedure, a call statement which triggers its execution, a statement which stops it within the procedure itself, and another one outside it for emergency purposes. Moreover, for a task, the artificial language includes a statement defining the priority of execution.

Example   A common function such as computing a logarithm is defined in most artificial languages and may be called as many times as is necessary.

Remark   A self-calling procedure is qualified as *recursive*. Many sentences in natural language of the type, 'do it again in the same way and again until . . .', corresponds to a reiteration of recursive calls. In particular the recursive relative access, and also sometimes the iterative relative access, are conveniently expressed by the recursive calling of an access procedure.

It is often useful to generalize a procedure by defining its execution with some entity values called *formal parameters* within the procedure. These formal parameters are replaced at the time of execution by values (variable expressions) known as *actual parameters*.

A procedure may also be generalized in its very nature. Only a pattern is described, a *generic procedure*, according to which a procedure is generated for particular circumstances.

Other statements

In this chapter we have seen how to define the general characteristics of actions in the way that they may be expressed using an artificial language conceived by an interlocutor of Indo-European idiom.

Some statements, however, are not intended for the processor itself but for the program translator (which is usually the same processor equipped with a utility program). Such statements are known as *translating instructions* and have an exclusive technical part.

Example   An instance is the order to produce as concise a translation as possible (this will be achieved at the expense of translation and execution durations).

A program also includes comments for the human reader of different points in the program. These comments are not orders but explanations or simply a means of spacing out presentation (*Figure 3.11*).

PROGRAM consisting of   *For the processor*
                                        orders in artificial language
                          For the translator
                                       instructions
                          For the human reader
                                       comments

Figure 3.11 Other statements

Chapter 4

Criteria of quality in software design

General and technical criteria

So far, we have looked at the nature of entities and actions, but not their *quality*.

Software designing is both complex and meticulous and so in order to set up rules that save us making random choices of entities and actions, we must define our general aims, namely our criteria of quality in software design.

Some of these criteria stem from mere common sense: they are *general criteria*. Others take into account the physical characteristics of the processors, sensors and effectors (the memories in particular) and are called *technical criteria* (*Figure 4.1*).

Note that the weight we put on a particular technical criterion may vary, as techniques improve. General criteria remain perennial, however.

General criterial of quality

Feasibility

The most direct criterion of quality in a design is for it to be feasible, that is, the problem must be stated accurately and a practically applicable algorithm of resolution must be known (*Figure 4.2*). This may seem almost too obvious to need stating, yet many designs come unstuck because of a lack of careful examination of the design's feasibility. This can cause serious problems which appear only when the study is more or less in the making.

Example The automatic translation of a natural language into another is not feasible, because there is no language whose syntactical and semantic rules are known accurately; they may even be intrinsically fuzzy. Similarly a large number of problems in operational research cannot be stated both accurately and

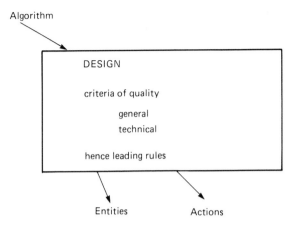

Figure 4.1 General and technical criteria

realistically. For instance, the problem of the best route for a delivery van – if traffic, rush hours, breakdown and driver's indisposition are taken into account – is eventually better solved, in complex cases, by human intuition and experience than by an over-simplifying algorithmic approach. That is why automatic translation and operational research programs have not met many optimistic expectations.

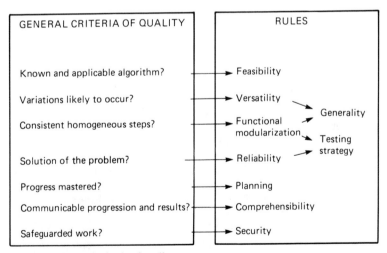

Figure 4.2 General criteria of quality

Feasibility rule   Any design must always be preceded by a study of its feasibility.

Versatility

Most problems evolve with time, either under the influence of alterations in their exterior constraints or because of new needs or desires. In particular, a satisfactory solution to a problem often prompts us to want to solve another more general or slightly different one. This is almost always the case in management – and very often, too, in scientific or technical computing – apart from a few mathematical problems.

It is therefore vital that, before starting the design proper, any possible variations are sought which are likely to have an impact on the problem to be solved.

Example   An alteration of the law concerning wages calculations, a new way of invoicing, a change of the limit conditions in the design of a technical part, the launching of a new sensor or effector, a weakening of the hypotheses in a mathematical problem are evolutions which urge us to completely or partly rewrite a design. As a matter of interest, it has been shown that more time is globally devoted to modifying existing designs and coding than to drafting new ones.

Versatility rule   Any design must be preceded by a study of its versatility (*Figure 4.2*).

Functional modularization and generality

The algorithms of real problems are usually complex, which means that either the entities or the actions or both require a long description. Only very repetitive algorithms may be simple while retaining a practical interest for designing and coding, but these are not the ones most frequently found. Determining entities, collections' organization and access, actions and collections of actions' structures is therefore difficult and cannot all be achieved simultaneously by the human mind (which can hardly encompass more than one item at a time).

Thus designing must be completed by breaking down each problem into well-defined partial problems and by repeating the process for each partial problem until they all become effectively easy to program. By a 'well-defined problem' we mean stating that we want to ensure a precise function that contributes to solving the initial problem. This enables us to keep, at each step of the design, such qualities as coherence and homogeneity.

Example Suppose we wish to turn a sum in digits (less than a thousand million) into its transcription in letters (say for the drafting of a cheque) in digits groups (units, hundreds, thousands, millions), and in a two-digits group for cents or pence. The first function will then consist in cutting up the sum into these groups; the second one in transcribing these groups in the proper order; the third one in placing, when necessary, the words million, thousand, dollars or pounds, sometimes 'zero dollar', or 'pound', cents or pence. The first and third functions are easy to design. Here is the second one: given the group of these numbers 'h, d, u', a subfunction links the transcriptions accordingly:

- to h, nothing, or 'A HUNDRED' or 'TWO HUNDRED',
  . . . or 'NINE HUNDRED'.;
- to d, nothing, or 'TEN', or 'TWENTY', . . . or 'NINETY';
- to u, nothing, or 'ONE' or 'TWO', . . . or 'NINE';
  Another subfunction chains those transcripts provided that this condition is fulfilled:
- if 10< 'du' <20, 'du' has a special correspondent, from

  'ELEVEN' to 'NINETEEN'

Rule of functional modularization The design must be carried out through a modularization of functions into subfunctions (until they become very simple) (*Figure 4.2*).

Simultaneously applying rules of versatility and functional modularization entails that, at each step, we must keep the function as general as possible, that is, choose the widest possible range of entities, entities' collections, actions and collections of actions' structures. (In fact, we only make a choice when we cannot go forward in any other way.)

Example In the transcription of a sum into letters, it is better to choose the word 'dollar' or 'pound' at the very last stage in case the design is used for other English-speaking countries with different currencies. It is also possible that the second function in the preceding example might be more intricate in other European languages, such as French.

This is the generality rule.

Reliability and the testing strategy rule

The design must eventually lead to a program solving the problem stated: this may also seem to be stating the obvious yet we seldom avoid mistakes if the problem is not very simple. So ensuring the reliability of the result implies some testing (*Figure 4.2*).

Example In the preceding problem, each function and subfunction must be tested separately.

Reliability rule The reliability of the design must be checked for evey function.

Simultaneously applying rules of functional modularization and reliability means that testing should take place as early as possible and for each step.

Example In the preceding design, it is advisable to check the first and third functions before the second one (which may be divided into subfunctions), even if only by hand.

This is the testing strategy rule.

Planning, comprehensibility and security

Carrying out the design takes time, usually several weeks or months, and thus mastering it implies planning the stages and scheduling them (*Figure 4.2*).

Remark Finding a real, or simply realistic, example of this is not easy, yet this rule is most important and should not be forgotten (except when a design only takes a few hours or days).

Planning rule Any large design should be planned.

Even though the result of the program design is a program executable by a machine, it is also (almost above everything else) a set of texts that human readers will have to understand so that it may be judged, altered, adapted, checked and corrected. It is rare that a program design does not have to be communicated to another person, since this would mean both that a single individual carried it out thoroughly and that the accuracy of the final results need not be checked or at least might be more easily checked by other means. So a program design must be sensible and clearly understandable in itself (*Figure 4.2*).

Example Maintenance problems, the existence of management frauds, the controversial character of many scientific or technical results arise mostly from the difficulty of understanding contrived or poorly documnented designs or programs.

Comprehensibility rule The design must read sensibly and be made explicit through updated, articulate documentation.

Lastly, designs, programs and entities are not only intellectual processes or abstract notions, devoid of value (expressed in monetary terms or otherwise) which might be carelessly dealt with and kept: they must be free from errors, malevolent intentions and frauds, that is, we must ensure their security (*Figure 4.2*).

Example Victims of breaches of security even if aware of the damage caused, may be hesitant to reveal it; data processing is doubtless a major domain of both crime and disastrous mistakes.

Security rule In its process and results, program designing should be protected by safety measures.

Remark Entities and actions cannot be intrinsically separated and should be designed simultaneously; however, in any organization of any size there are often a great number of entities (usually gathered into one or several data bases) and applications. If the design is correct, each of the applications is fairly independent of the other ones so that their set is of additive, not multiplicative, complexity. This is not the case for entities which are often common to several applications.

Example The number of unbooked seats on each flight of an airline company are entities common to all the queries, reservations and sales.

These entities are not recreated and manipulated by each of the applications because, beside the minor problem of redundancy (lost space), the coherence of the manipulations would imply that each change in value be instantaneously reverberated on each of the copies. So a particular function is chosen which deals with the exclusive management of the data base, and the varied applications manipulate entities only by calling that function. This is, rather inappropriately, called *independence of programs and data*.

Example In the preceding example, there is no risk of selling the same seat several times simultaneously if only one function is entitled to authorize the sale.

Technical criteria of quality

Classification

Naturally, technical criteria are uppermost in a program designer's mind when trying to tackle a problem. Yet these are far less important, even from a practical viewpoint, than the general rules discussed above.

Remark Statistics have shown that designers aiming at solving technical restraints (a pseudo-optimization in particular) produce codes that are less versatile, coherent, reliable and well-mastered than those who virtually forget about factual difficulties as much as they can. In addition, their designs on average, cost twice as much and give a poorer result.

When the decision of solving a problem automatically (a well-defined one with at least one solution algorithm being known), is either being examined, or already made, only two questions are raised (*Figure 4.3*):

● are we sure to get results (that is a program supplying the results expected)?

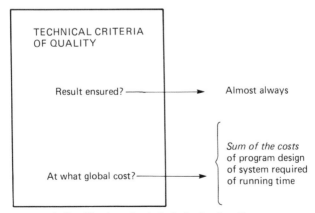

Figure 4.3 Classification of technical criteria of quality

● how much will it cost? Whatever the economic regime and even if the cost is computed in work-days (a rather an idealistic point of view that may be acceptable only in wealthy research institutes).

Historically, the first question remained relevant for a long time because, for many algorithms, the design could not lead to programs adapted to the available machines. Nowadays, machines' abilities are so wide-ranging that, apart from a few exceptions, the difficulties of solving a problem are either due to the lack of algorithms (with which software design is not concerned) or high cost, so only the second question is still valid (and will always remain so).

Example   We may compute to millions of decimals the value of π, solve all the well-defined management problems automatically, efficiently control the route of a rocket, thoroughly compute the characteristics of a tower, and so on. However, this may not always be worthwhile. For example, a study of the swell motions and the deposit of alluvions carried out before building a harbour is better done on a model than by computing.

The second question, that of cost, can be subdivided into the following, interdependent costs:

● that of the program design;
● that of the required system, that is, the processor, its sensors and effectors (in particular, the cost of the memories) and the utility programs it may be equipped with;
● that of the running time, which itself depends on the quality of the program design and the abilities of the system.

The first two costs will now be examined successively, together with the third one as it depends on them.

Cost of the program design (languages)

Although choosing between several algorithms (where this is possible) is not directly relevant to program design, its importance as a factor in fast design, system required and running time should not be overlooked (*Figure 4.4*). Sometimes one algorithm is better than another one in all these respects simultaneously; it should then naturally be chosen, even if it requires more initial thinking.

Example   Let us assume we have to calculate the number of partitions of an integer n, that is, the number of ways of writing

Costs

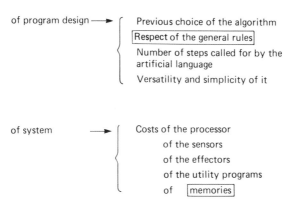

of running time

Figure 4.4 Costs of program design and systems

it as a sum of at most *n* positive integers. (This could be useful in, say, dividing a load into different parcels.) The principle of a first algorithm may be to try all the possible cases by evaluating them, but this gives designing and, more important, running times that are far too long.

A second algorithm, less obvious at first sight, consists of the following:

Let $p(n, m)$ be the number of ways for writing *n* as the sum of at most *m* integers; then $p(n, m) = p(n, m - 1) + p(n - m, m)$ as this relation when defined ($n, m - 1, n - m$ and *m* positive) means there are as many ways of writing *n* as a sum of *m* integers at most as of writing it with $m - 1$ integers increased with the numbers of ways of writing it with *m* integers exactly (given a sum equal to *n* of *m* integers exactly), by taking 1 off each term, we get a sum equal to $n - m$ of at most *m* terms and conversely. There are thus $p(n - m, m)$ sums of this type. And $p(n, m)$ has to be computed directly if $m = 1$, for $p(n, m - 1)$ has no meaning, yielding $p(n, 1) = 1$; or if $n - m < 1$, that is $n \leq m$, for $p(n - m, m)$ has no meaning, yielding $p(n, m) = p(n, n)$.

Although one algorithm may appear better than another from one viewpoint this may not be so from another. Thus in order to choose the better algorithm, we must make a balanced estimate of the costs involved.

Example   To evaluate the integral of a function f from a to b, we may choose the first following algorithm, as it is easy to design. Let the segment (a, b) be divided into n equal steps (n being set outside the design). The value of f is calculated at each end of the steps and a weighted sum is computed (for instance, using weights of 1 at any point except a and b where the sum is weighted by $\frac{1}{2}$, or alternatively of $\frac{3}{4}$ and $\frac{2}{3}$, except at a and b where the weight is $\frac{1}{3}$.)

A second algorithm may be chosen. A first approximation of the integral is computed by $[f(a) + f(b)]\ [(b - a)/2]$ and a second one by $\{[f(a)/2] + [f(a/2 + b/2)] + [f(b)/2)\ ]\ [(b - a)/2]$. If the difference between the approximations is significant, the same operation is made simultaneously on the segments $[a, (a + b)/2]$ and $[(a + b)/2, b]$.

The choice of the best algorithm is related to the possibility of determining n; this is feasible for a function which varies regularly, but not when it shows unknown or extremely variable convexities or concavities. Then, and only then, is the second self-adaptive algorithm preferable.

Sometimes the algorithm is prescribed by its uniqueness.

Example   Here is the problem of the Hanoi towers. Let there be three vertical poles i, j, k and n pierced discs, all of different sizes, piled up on one pole from the largest beneath to the smallest on top. The whole pile has to be transferred on to another pole, disc by disc, so that, at each step, the discs should be displayed on the three poles without any disc being placed on a smaller one. This problem is practically solvable only through the algorithm whose principle is based on the remark that, in order to take n discs from pole i to pole j, it is sufficient to take $n - 1$ discs from pole i to pole k, then the remaining disc from pole i to pole j and finally the $n - 1$ discs from pole k to pole j and the process repeated. The algorithm of transfer of n discs from pole i to pole j is then:

- immediate if $n = 1$,
- otherwise $n - 1$ discs have to be transferred from i to k, then 1 from i to j, lastly $n - 1$ from k to j.

Ultimately an algorithm may be imposed by conditions irrelevant to the cost of program design, so making its choice outside the realm of software design.

Example In numerical analysis, computing eigenvalues of a matrix may be affected by various methods, according to the nature of the matrix and the accuracy required for the results. Similarly, the computation of a tax is totally determined by exterior rules.

Once an algorithm has been chosen, the cost of the program design depends on:

- respecting the general rules of feasibility, versatility, functional modularization, reliability, planning and documentation mentioned earlier in this chapter and the application of which is dealt with later;
- the eventual degree of accuracy required to launch into coding, that is, the number of necessary intermediate stages.

Languages

This number of stages depends directly on the different existing *artificial languages*, which, more or less successfully, express the descriptions of entities, collections and accesses, actions and their structures. By 'artificial languages' we mean the tools for both file and data base management and the tools used to translate the writing of statements (the translators of programming languages proper), usually performed by distinct utility programs but which the programmer can encompass as one.

Unfortunately, most systems of file and data base management offer only primitive facilities on a given machine.

Example A data base management system can often deal only with hierarchical organization; such a file management system can perform only an absolute access; or such a language cannot convey the making-up of a group of items of information.

Besides, even the so-called high-level programming languages often lack a structure for the most natural statements and actions.

Example Such a language cannot express the conditional statement: when . . ., when . . ., when . . .; others are unable to form a block; others can say: do . . . while . . ., but not: do . . . until . . .; and so on.

So we are still far from having reached the ideal: an artificial language with rich semantics and few syntactic constraints.

The present state of affairs has historical causes which are nevertheless not without solution: primitive ideas due to a relative novelty of the techniques and also of the attitude of many senior people in the software field whose minds are closed to new ideas.

This does not prevent the more recently trained users from evermore using and advocating natural and powerful tools, for awareness of implied costs (as well as of the tediousness of using primitive artificial languages) keeps increasing.

Nevertheless the practical solution is not to construct one's design according to the tools available (since this would contradict the general rules and is not justified from an economic viewpoint), but to translate by hand, in the final stages, a correct design in keeping with the tools available.

Remark   The expression *programming languages* should strictly apply only to modern artificial languages, conceived to word a correct design without too many contrivances. The term *coding languages* refers to older languages that refer explicitly to particular machines and often require technical knowledge.

In some simple cases however, it may be preferable from a practical angle, to consider the tool first, but an estimation of the cost involved has to be made.

Example   The highest common factor (HCF) of two integers m and n may be determined by a recursive algorithm (which, incidentally, is its mathematical definition):

- if n is zero, it is m;
- otherwise, it is the HCF of n and the remainder of the division of m by n.

But for a language not equipped with the recursive calling of a procedure, immediately converting the definition into an iterative design is advisable.

The cost of programming itself depends on the richness of the artificial language and the simplicity of its syntax (a difficult compromise for the originators of a language). Both of these are extremely variable, many languages being fit for use in one type of application only (management or science, for instance).

Example   One artificial language may call a procedure only by a complex and dangerous transfer method; another may accept

only few lettered identifiers which are then generally incompre-
hensible; many languages are, by themselves, unable to take
time and events into account or to handle errors, and they imply
calling procedures written in other languages; recursive calling,
however natural and useful it may be, is often missing or leads to
copying a procedure by calling (which soon becomes prohibitive).

However, in a correctly designed program with checking stages,
programming is not the highest cost.

Cost of the necessary system

The cost of a system required for running a program is the total
costs of the processor, its sensors and effectors (the memories in
particular) and the utility programs with which it is equipped.

Processors, sensors and effectors

The processor is characterized by the number and nature of its
primitive actions (elementary instruction set), the running time
needed for them, the size of the inner memory, and its own utility
programs (operating systems). but it is chosen according to
management criteria outside the field of the program designers as
such (and, consequently, of software design). The designer can
only expect to limit the space necessary within the memory
through a reduction of the numbers of actions and entities.
However, it is often pointless to spend time reducing memory
usage, because, besides the directly increased cost of program
design, the general criteria (in particular, comprehensibility and
versatility) tend to be disregarded in the process.

Example It may seem awkward to keep a whole collection of
data which are definitely processed one after the other; but it
would be worse to re-use the same entity with different
meanings in order to minimize memory usage.

The sensors and effectors (except the memories) are also
outside the realm of software design for, like the processor, they
are usually chosen according to technical or management priorities
and not deduced from the design for a given application.

Example A printer has its printing speed determined by the
global volume of print in a centre, and it is almost always dealt

with by the operating system and not, directly, by the programmer.

The fact that processors, sensors and effectors are outside the field of software design does not mean that a design programmer is necessarily unaware of their characteristics, but that they usually have no influence upon his methodological options.

Example   The technical characteristics of a sensor (a measuring instrument), for instance the noises (random fluctuations) which may affect measurement, are of great importance for the program design in an industrial environment.

Conversely, the organization of entities' collections and their access are always widely or totally controlled by program designers. For data base management systems, there often exists one task (data base administration) carried out by specialists, who may be considered functionally as particular users since they construct the core part of the work.

Types of memory

There are three functional types of memory (*Figure 4.5*):

*   the first one permits access by the entity's name. For example, the inner memory of the processor which enables the actions to call well-identified entities by their names. These are known as the *symbolic memories*;
*   the second type of memory permits access by value: the present fastest memories belong to this category. They are known as the *associative memories*. Of course we do not try to access on information that is entirely known, but a partial value of it that is known;
*   the third type of memory permits neither access by name nor access by value: the memories are divided into well-ordered cells each one of which is accessible through indicating its call-number or address. The large current memories are of this type and are known as the *addressing memories*.

Remark   The memory of the first type is, in its technical form, the same as the second or more often third type, but the access time is so fast that the user may conveniently ignore it. The memories of the second type consist of fixed of circulating cells (the record being then selected dynamically). A distinction is that memories

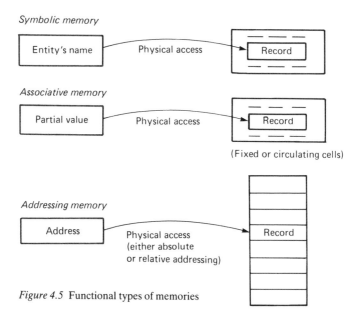

Figure 4.5 Functional types of memories

of the third type have an access time that either does not depend much on the address (random access memories) or, conversely is very dependent upon it, such as the memories where we can access from the cell of address n to that of address m only through a previous access to all the intermediates from n to m. These memories, called sequential access memories, are differentiated by the respective terms of *absolute addressing* and *relative addressing*.

Conversion from logical access to physical access

Such accesses are called *physical* as they are conditioned by the nature of the memory, whereas *logical* accesses are conceptual and result from the design.

As we have seen, we cannot call one or several records in a collection by its or their names but only through an absolute or relative access by value or an iterative or recursive relative access and, in the latter case, with the aid of either a pointer or a key.

So, when the collection is in an associative memory, the access by value is immediate, whereas the access by pointer requires the translation *pointer towards value*, and the access by key supplies a whole subcollection (except if the key is characteristic of a single record) which takes us back to the same general problem.

When the collection is in an addressing memory, the access by value requires the translation *value towards address*, whereas the access by pointer requires the translation *pointer towards address* and the access by key requires the translation *key towards address*, which is not distinct from the translation *value towards address* (*Figure 4.6*).

These translations are not all fast and easy; the program designer must therefore be aware of the existence of technical criteria of organization and access as well as of the translating methods.

In particular, a file in a heap is easily dealt with as such only in an associative memory; otherwise it usually has to have been previously organized, that it, ordered into a chained list by a pointer or a key or sorted. A file organized as a chain can be fairly easily dealt with in an addressing memory, but in an associative memory, it requires a second extraction from the subcollection to yield a precise record.

A network base is fairly simply dealt with exclusively in an addressing memory, as the access there is mostly effected by pointers.

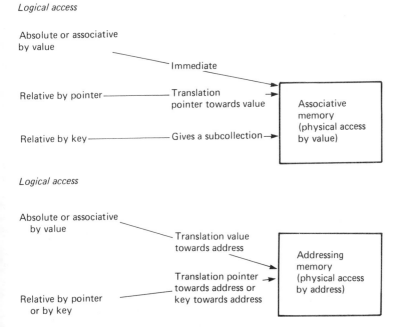

Figure 4.6 Access to a record in a collection

A relational base is conveniently processed exclusively in an associative memory, as the access there is mostly effected by keys. Actually the problem of sorting a relational base is limited to that of only one logical file, so it is not distinct.

Remark   A file is often called internal if it is in an inner memory or external if it is in an outer memory (or has only a virtual existence, as it consists of records received by a sensor or sent to an effector. This distinction is not useful functionally but only practically (because the capacities and times of access are not the same), except if the functional types of the memories are different.

A sensor or an effector through which communication is made by sending well-order items of information is functionally equivalent to an addressing memory, where the different exchange times play the role of positions. In practical terms, a data base is always in an outer memory.

Conclusion

The topics we have covered in this chapter should now enable us, from a practical point of view, to define those subjects (*Figure 4.7*) to which we should pay close attention in the program design of a given algorithm intended to result in the execution of a program by a given system (including its artificial language).

The choice of the organization and access of the entities should take into account specifically:
- the translation pointer towards value,
- the translation value towards address, or key towards address,
- the translation pointer towards address,
- the way of sorting a heap by a pointer or a key.

Remark   A name may be assimilated to a value as it may be considered as the instantiation of a record in a file of identifiers; thus the problem of translation name towards address is not specific.

Program design should be carried out so as to respect the general rules of:
- feasibility,
- versatility,

- functional modularization,
- generality,
- reliability,
- checking strategies,
- planning,
- comprehensibility,
- security.

Unfortunately all those subjects are not independent.

Choice of organization and access:

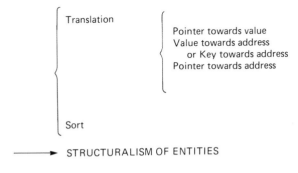

STRUCTURALISM OF ENTITIES

Carrying out of program design

General rules

STRUCTURALISM OF ACTIONS

Figure 4.7 Conclusion

Example   The problem of access to a word in a dictionary in an addressing memory where every term appears followed by its definitions may be dealt with in one of the following three ways:

- By a previous sorting, ordering it by a decreasing retrieval occurrence and an organization in a chain where we access until we come upon the word required. The process of the program design is commonplace and the program will be excellent as regards the general rules, but the organization and mode of access are disastrous if the words are numerous and the retrieval occurrence does not decrease very fast.

- By a previous sorting in alphabetical order and a translation value (of the word) towards address performed in this way. We compute the address of the word in the middle in the dictionary (to the nearest half if the number of words is even), then we reiterate within the half where the word is, and so on until the word in the middle is the one required. The process of the design is slightly more difficult but the organization and access are usually not as bad as above.
- By a hierarchical organization where each record possesses as value the first letters common to all its descendants, the descendants being empty or built in the same way. The program proves much harder to build up but the organization and access are generally the best.

Chapter 5

Structuralism of entities

Introduction

We have seen that the logical access to an entity in a collection can be either:

- by value (and thus absolute or associative);
- or by relative (and thus iterative or recursive).

We have also seen that the organization of a file can be either:

- not actual (when it is a heap and access is by value);
- or in a graph (more particularly in a chain, the relations between records being marked by pointers or keys, and access then being relative. In the case of keys, it is not basically distinct from the access by value).

We have also seen that a data base can be organized either:

- in a network or plex (in particular hierarchically; the relations are then mostly marked by pointers and consequently access is relative);
- or as a relational base (the relations being mostly marked by keys, access consequently being by value).

Lastly we have seen that memories make physical access possible:

- by name (which poses no important or specific problems);
- or by value (which causes problems of translation from pointer towards value, or key towards value for the files in a graph, the latter appearing also in network bases);
- or by absolute or relative address (which creates problems of translation from pointer towards address or key towards address for the file in a graph and the network bases and in translating value towards address for the files in a heap, which can often be avoided by previous sorting, and the relational bases. This last problem does not differ significantly from that of translating key towards address).

Types of entities' structure

Table and network structures and typology

The organizations, the logical and physical accesses and the translations are shown in *Figure 5.1*.

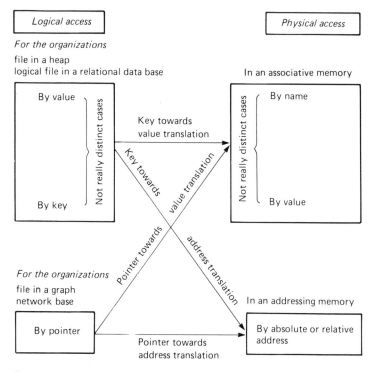

Figure 5.1 Organizations, logical and physical accesses and translations

We shall now simplify the terminology by calling:

- *table structure*, any organization where logical access is completed through one or several keys without any further distinction between value and key;
- *network or plex structure*, any organization where logical access is achieved through one or several pointers (*Figure 5.2*).

We shall not distinguish between access by value and access by name, and the latter expression will no longer be used.

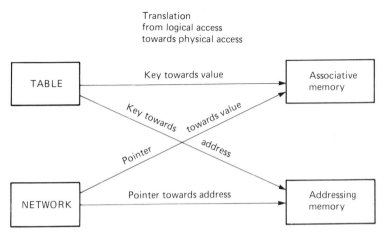

Figure 5.2 Simplified terminology

Such a simplification enables us to describe the organizations and logical access in a more general way. Now we are able to describe any organization and any access, however complex they may be, by using the following terms only: table, key, network and pointer.

Example In a previous example we looked at a university described by two logical files in a relational base: professors and the lectures they gave, and students and the lectures they attended. Every lecture given may now be accompanied by a pointer designating the first student enrolled (according to any order); every lecture attended is now accompanied by a pointer towards the next student (in the same order as the chosen one), the pointer for the last student going back to the lecture attended. The description of this organization which, while not really complicated is still not particularly simple, can be reduced to this: table of professors and lectures given, table of students and lectures attended, network of students enrolled for a lecture given. The problems of access and translation are very general, which is not obvious at first sight.

The preceding classification advantageously simplifies our text, and widens the range of algorithms, designs and codings that describe the organization of the entities and ensure proper access to them. In addition, it enables us to get rid of merely technical and often extremely variable considerations and terminologies.

For instance the description of a record – usually nothing more than a hierarchical micro-organization of groups – is usually intended for the independent translator of the programming language, that of the file organization is meant for the file-management system and that of a base (in this case often called conceptual schema) is intended for the translator of a data description language which belongs to the data base management system.

Similarly, the access to a record is usually completed by the result of the translated program linked either to some routines in the file management system which can almost be considered as ordinary subprograms, or to statements intended for the data-manipulation language translator, which belongs to the data base management system too.

Lastly, the description of translation problems is freed from purely physical options which are usually solved (at least partly) by the file or data base management systems (then globally called internal schema): actual layout of the records in the file, of the files in the memory or memories, of the data bases in one or several locations, distribution of the reliability and security tests, actual presence of a file in a data base or transparency of it on request, the transfer of records between outer and inner memories and so on.

It is clear that the programmer must know something of these problems, but it is certain that precise answers can only be found in the hardware and software suppliers' manuals or as a result of common sense, experience and simulations.

Example Suppose we physically keep a collection of entities, each consisting of a person's identity, his or her address and current bank-account number. The collection may consist of full record after full record or a record of pointer only, the first pointer showing the full name, the second showing the address and the following ones each fragment of the bank-account number. It will then become useless to keep, say, an address for each person; each occurrence of a new address will be sufficient. Even though technical considerations and common sense only enable us to choose between one layout or the other, both organization and access can be described in general terms.

The preceding typology helps us to separate the conceptual aspect from the technical one and also takes into account single entities as well as collections of entities.

Difficulty of choosing entities' structure

Eventually the different organizations are reduced to broad categories, no one of which is clearly understandable or natural.

As regards the structure of entities in program design, the ultimate aim is to avoid any mistakes in principle, that is to find the best structure in the program design. The human mind does not take to this easily and so there is a major difficulty in choosing, especially where technical rules play the largest role. As a consequence, the following part of this chapter will be descriptive.

Table structure

Definitions: tables, keys, arrays, indices and vectors

A *table* is a file of records representing varied instantiations of the same entity, where logical access is provided by one or several keys.

Example   A file of people where certain keys permit access (such as surname, first and second names) or with just one key (for example bank account number) is a table. (Note that in the first case only there may be homonyms.)

In the particular case where all keys are integers (positive, negative or zero), each of which is included between two limits and, moreover, where each set of such numbers points to an actual record (provided the limits are taken into account), the table is then specifically called an *array*, and the keys, *indices*.

Example   A rectangular array could be produced for, say, output of products manufactured in the last ten years in the main towns of a country numbered from one to fifty; a triangular array of the distances between the main towns determined by the same matriculations (as an index is delimited as a function of another one, the limit may vary, but the main point is that there be no blanks).

Remark   The common meaning for the word 'table' is often an array, for example a logarithmic table.

The primitives of access – creation, updating and cancellation – as well as the enquiry about its existence may be expressed without ambiguity if and only if the chosen keys permit access to a single value. Consequently, this is what is sought, with the result reading unambiguously on an array. The enquiry about contents is also expressed with some keys but access to a single record is not always guaranteed.

Example   In the preceding file of individuals, updating the address would not be convenient if only the keys 'surname, first name and second name' were used, because we may come upon homonyms. If it proves easier for a practical reason, it is possible to access the subset of homonyms through the name, then within it to seek further if it is not reduced to one record.

Remark   An array with a single index is called a *vector*. The number of possible values of the index, that is, of the elements of the vector, is called its size. The two primitive of access 'first' and 'last' may be added for convenience. These are expressed as a function of the name of the 'vector' entity (and not of the index), and point respectively to the records from the lowest to the highest index. Obviously creating and cancelling records, in a vector, can be completed only at the ends.

Logical access and translations

Direct, calculation and scattered access

When a table is in an associative memory, a logical access must perform a key-towards-value translation, that is, give the keys a characteristic value for the memory. We can proceed:

- at once, by concatenation (linking together) of the keys (or some fragments of them) when this enables us to get such a value;
- by logical or set-like calculation when a combining of the keys (through the operators) leads to the same result;
- by one or the other of the two ways above, so as to get a subset in which a new different access will be necessary when no concatenation or known calculation can supply a characteristic value (*Figure 5.3*).

Example   In a library we may have to locate a record by a key consisting of numbers and letters (including, for instance, the last two digits of the publishing year, the first five letters of the author's name, and an extra order number avoiding problems of homonymy), plus a key consisting of the main author's name and a further few key words mentioning the topics dealt with. In

Entity

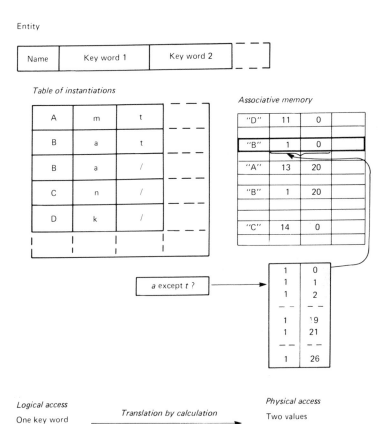

Figure 5.3 Key towards value translation

those conditions, a reader knowing the key would access a document at once. However, often he knows only the author's name or maybe even a few key words: that is why all the documentary languages enable us to compute logical relations between these key words, author's name and date (by 'and', 'or', 'except', etc.), which produces a sub-collection in which the enquiry is carried out further by new accesses.

The only precautions to be taken are not to create any ambiguity (a key value already there) and not to update or cancel a subcollection when a single record is changed.

- by building up a dictionary of the translations, called an index, setting up correspondences between the keys and characteristic values: but it is simpler to make the keys appear in the record and use them directly.

Remark The translation problem cannot be tackled the other way round, by exploring the memory value after value until the required record sought by the keys is found. This is because on average it would be necessary to explore half the file in order to access the record and to keep a file of the instantiated values. The table organization would then be more of a hindrance than a help.

When a table is in an addressing memory, a logical access must perform a key-towards-address absolute or relative translation. We proceed as follows:

- At once by concatenating the keys (or some fragments of them) when we can obtain an absolute address, such an access is called *direct* and is very simple and fast, and enables us to dispense with the key in the record in the memory. However, it is rarely feasible as the choices between keys have to be free (that is, arbitrary choosing) easy to alter (to allow transfer from one memory to another), and their value range must show only a few blanks (otherwise a significant part of the memory is allocated but not used).

Example If a memory is such that each cell is addressed by the juxtaposition of a first number from 1 to 1024 and of a second one from 1 to 256, we may imagine placing a file there with a thousand entities, each of which occupies at most 256 cells, and choosing the first number for a key. However, a lot of space may be lost and, above all, a change of memory may be disastrous, like an increase in the number of records or even a drift in the numbering (creation of new records, some older ones being cancelled at random).

- By calculation (numerical or similar) when certain operations on the keys lead to the same result. This is easy for a simple-shaped array (rectangle, triangle, strip in the shape of a parallelogram) and simple for a vector in particular; otherwise it is not very difficult to find a simple way of computing which may establish a relation between keys and address without too many blanks. It is, however, almost impossible not to cause *collisions*, that is, we cannot avoid the calculation leading to the same results for different values of keys (then called *synonyms*. Such an access is called *calculated* or *scattered* and so cannot generally be used alone.

Example   In order to identify a hundred thousand people among a country's population, excluding any person aged 100 or over, we may imagine a single key per person consisting of:

- the number 1 if male, 2 if female;
- two digits, the last ones of the year of birth (00 to 99);
- the two digits of the month of birth (01 to 12);
- the two digits of the day of the month of birth (01 to 31 at most);
- four digits similar to the postal code of the place of birth;
- two digits indicating the order of birth of people born on the same day at the same place;

But this key has thirteen numbers, there are ten thousand billion possibilities, and it is therefore impracticable to devote one cell to every possible number. But whatever key fragments are retained, calculations done and adding of characteristic elements of the name performed, we cannot be safe from collisions. For instance, taking the last five numbers and the first letter of the name leads us to use only the twentysixth of the place blocked and does not even solve the difficulty.

Remark   The actual order of the records in memory (that is, the order as decreed by the address) has no apparent meaning, for it does not appear to be linked with any key as long as the calculation of the address has not be remade.

Sequential access

We could proceed by encompassing the translation problem in another way, by exploring the memory, address after address, until the required record is found by the keys (then included in the record). This access is called *sequential* and must avoid unoccupied cells. It entails exploring half the file on average in order to access a record, so it is used alone only if a major part (or the whole) of the file is to be processed. There is a drawback to this in that the records are found in a random order, except if formerly sorted out on a key.

Indexed accesses

We can build up a dictionary of the translations, called an *index*, which is itself either a table consisting of the keys and the corresponding addresses or a network with the same function. The space taken is then considerably increased (sometimes the index may be more cumbersome than the file) and this access is worthwhile only when the index may be organized either as a vector on one of the keys (with, if necessary, a few blanks in the key sequence, the translation of which is replaced by a value of address known as impossible to occur), or as it will be seen later, in a tree structure. Moreover, several indexes would often have to be created, a borderline case being one for every key. That is why such an access, called *indexed* is seldom used alone.

So, generally speaking, the direct translation is not feasible, the scattered one causes collisions, the sequential one is awkward, and the indexed one does not simplify much.

Collision and overflow

A first compromise consists in using, in spite of its disadvantages, the principle of a scattered access, but taking special steps whenever a collision occurs when records are created (*Figure 5.4*). In that case we can locate the synonym:

- in the first space available found through sequential retrieval (this implies another displacing of the synonym, if this space is needed later);
- in a space calculated as a function of that where the collision took place (this solution is called *iterative* and does not exclude another collision). Thus each series of synonyms makes up a table where access is completed through a cascade of calculated accesses;
- in any space whose location is kept in a pointer associated with the record (linking of synonyms);
- in any space whose location is kept in an index of keys and positions of each synonym associated to the record; time is then gained at the expense of space.

For all the accesses other than for creation, we must check that the required record actually is in the calculated location – the most frequent case if the chosen solution has proved a good one – and in the reverse case, we must seek it in the same way as for the access for creation.

We may also preserve a special overflow area where all the synonyms are placed:

- in the first space available. Simultaneously, an indicator signalling to the ulterior accesses the presence of at least one

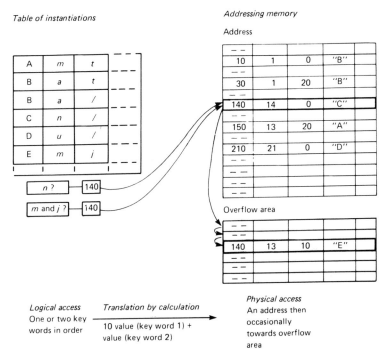

Figure 5.4 Key towards address translation. First compromise with overflow area in case of collision

collision (and the necessity of a search in the overflow area) accompanies the record already placed in the calculated space, so the ulterior accesses will explore the overflow area in a sequence, which may be feasible only when it remains fairly limited;
- in any space, like the linking of synonyms;
- in a space calculated or kept in an index, but this becomes very awkward.

Segmented access

A second compromise consists in still using the scattered access principle, but by calculating the address of an area or *segment* and not of an elementary position. Within each area the access to the records may be sequential or indexed: this segmented access thus multiplies the number of collisions, but reduces the disadvantage of each of them (*Figure 5.5*).

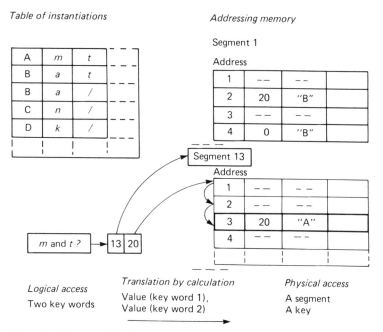

Figure 5.5 Key towards address translation. Second compromise: segmented organization

The two preceding compromises are not flexible, because a file cannot be reorganized, that is, taking it up and copying it in the same organization leaves the average number of collisions unchanged. Yet there is a wide range of practical choices (of the accurate method, the iteration calculation, the length of the area, etc.) which can be evaluated only by simulation for a given file.

Indexed sequential access

A third compromise consists in combining an indexed access applying to segments and a sequential access in each segment, with an extra overflow area (*Figures 5.6* and *5.7*).

Such organizations are called *indexed sequential* and offer many variants, one of which usually appears in a file management system (designed independently of the particular applications and consequently not optimized for a given file).

The file is segmented, and each segmnent can be subdivided into areas. All the keys are well ordered, a major index pointing (for each segment) to the highest value of the keys corresponding to

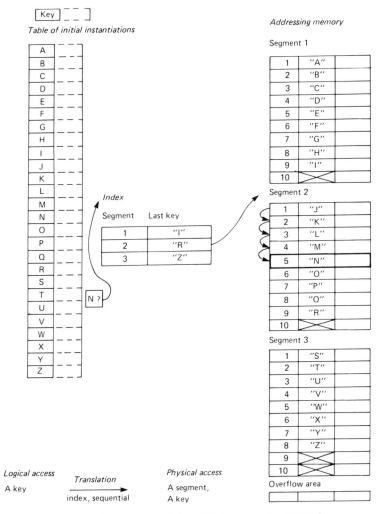

Figure 5.6 Key towards address translation. Third compromise: indexed
sequential; creation and access before insertions

the actual records (within the segment), and in each segment a
minor index plays the same role for each of the areas.

The major index, then the minor one, are examined; when the
area in which access must be completed is thus known, access may
be achieved by any method, usually the sequential one (which
explains the name of the organization: indexed then sequential).

The creation, from a file ordered following the values of the
keys, causes no difficulty, but when insertions overflow an area,

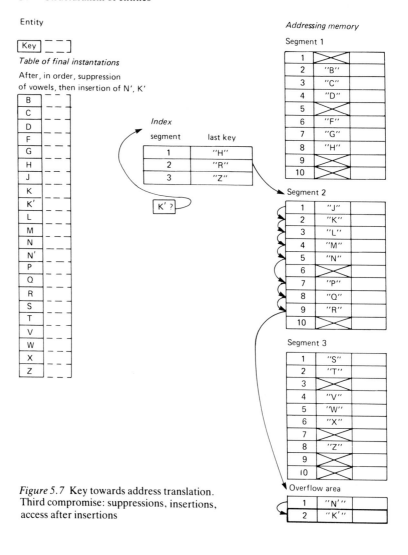

Entity

Addressing memory

Figure 5.7 Key towards address translation.
Third compromise: suppressions, insertions,
access after insertions

the latest records are pushed forward into an overflow area (for
example, organized in chains that physically intermingle but are
each linked to an area).

Remark   The major index usually is in an inner memory; and the
segments and areas usually have a physical reality (cylinders and
tracks).

The efficiency of such an organization depends on the practical choices made (rate of initial filling of the areas, number of segments, etc.).

The access is fast when the overflow area is small. When this is not the case, the file has to be recreated according to the same principle and by reading it in the order of the keys.

All the accesses that are not immediate are called indirect.

Types of table

The table structure does not offer a wide range of choices; it is adapted for records that are loosely linked together.

Network structure

Definitions: pointer, tree structure, node, root and chain

A *network* is a file of records showing varied instantiations of entities, where logical access is performed by one or several *pointers*.

Example A set of known relatives and parents could be organized in a network, with a pointer for each married person and pointers for each direct descendant or ascendant. A set of studies dealing with closely related subjects is also organized in a network with the aid of bibliographies where each author quotes his sources.

When the records are of the same kind and have a fixed maximal number of descendants, it is often convenient to consider that they all possess that maximal number of descendants exactly, and to give all the pointers which do not actually refer to one, one same predefined value called the *nil pointer*.

Example In the preceding network of people, each record will have two pointers towards the direct ascendants, but if any of them is unknown, its corresponding pointers will have a particular predefined value: an algorithm of retrieval of the ascendants will be simplified at the cost of a test of actual existence.

In the particular case when all the records belong to the same type and each of them has one single direct ascendant, except one record called the *top* or *root* which has none, the network is called a *tree structure*.

Example   A person's father and mother, his four grandparents, and so on for all the known ancestors build up a tree structure (where the ascendant in the structure meaning is the descendant in the genealogy background), except if we go high enough to find a common ancestor for two people married together.

The *primitives of access* – creation, updating and suppressing, the *question of actual presence*, the *inquiry about contents* – are unambiguously expressed with the aid of pointers; there is no access to subcollections as there may sometimes occur with tables.

Example   The pointer referring to the father in the preceding example.

Remark   A tree structure is called *binary* when each record has two descendants at most; this case deserves consideration in practice in compiling, memorizing dictionaries, etc. In that case it is convenient to express the primitives of access – question of actual presence and inquiry about contents – with the specific names of left and right pointers, and sometimes to add a primitive of access 'brother' which refers to the other direct ascendant's descendant, if any. The access to the root is completed by referring to the name of the entity, of which the records are instantiations. These are called *nodes* (often even when the network is not a binary tree structure).

Example   The preceeding tree structure.

Remark   A tree structure where each record has one and only one descendant except the last one is called a *chain*, each record is then called a *link*. This case is very important in practice. The root and the last record are then conveniently called by the specific names of *header record* and *last entry*, and a primitive of *linking* is added, relating to the last entry of a first chain to the header record of a second one. The words 'list' or 'chained list' are usually considered as synonyms for 'chain'. In a chain no primitive of access enables us to go back to the preceeding record. A chain is called *empty* if the access to the head gives a nil-pointer value.

Example   In a chain, inserting a record referred to by P between two others respectively pointed to by R and S is done that way, the order being significant:

- chain P and S (link the subchain whose head is S to the last entry pointed to by P);
- chain R and P (that is, link the subchain whose last record is R to the record pointed to by P).

Similarly, to add an item after the last record of the chain whose last significant pointer is T, is done in the following way, in any order:

- give the nil-pointer value to the follower of the record pointed to by P;
- chain T and P.

To add an item before the header record of a chain may be done in the following way and here the order is significant:

- chain P and the pointer at the head;
- give value P to the pointer at the head.

Lastly, to suppress the record pointed to by S and placed between the one pointed to by R and the other pointed to by T is done like this:

- chain R and T (that is, give the value T to the pointer referring to the follower of R).

Updatings are thus very simple.

Logical access and translations

Immediate or calculated access

When a network is in an associative memory, a logical access must achieve a pointer towards value translation, that is establish a correspondence between the pointers and a characteristic value in the memory. (*Figure 5.8*). We may proceed:

- at once by concatenating pointers or some fragments of them, if we can get a single characteristic value in that way;
- by calculation if combining pointers through operators leads to the same result;
- by building up a dictionary of the translations, called an index, establishing a correspondence between the pointers and a characteristic value.

In all those cases pointers play a role similar to that of keys and the translation problems are not distinct.

Entity

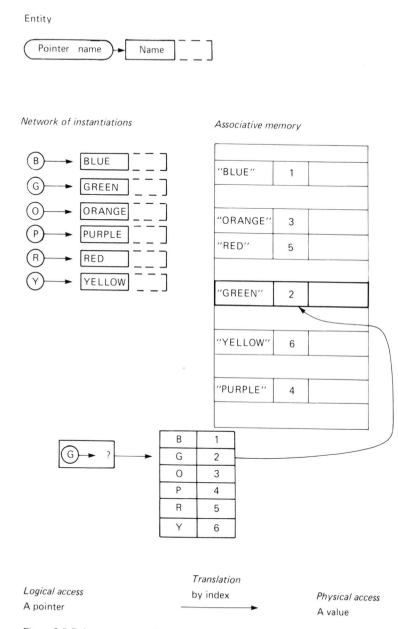

Figure 5.8 Pointer towards value translation

Remark   We cannot deal with the translation problem the other way round, by exploring the memory value after value until retrieving the record sought by the pointers, because, on average, half the file would have to be explored so as to access a record and we would have to keep a file of the instantiated values; the network organization would then be more of a hindrance than a help.

When a network is in an addressing memory, a logical access must perform a pointer-towards-address (whether absolute or relative) translation. We may proceed as follows.

- At once if the pointer is a physical absolute or relative address. This access is very simple and fast and used very frequently. Its advantage is to completely dissociate the logical aspect and the physical one. Consequently it is very suitable for updatings and easy transfer from one memory to another (at the cost, for the absolute address, of a conversion of the pointers, which does not change anything in the algorithms). In the case of a chain, a relative pointer may even be suppressed if the storage into memory is consecutive, in order of the links, and if the additions and suppressions are done at the ends (cancellations may also be achieved elsewhere by marking nil values, but no addition may be done without a reordering).
  It is often profitable to devote a whole memory area to a file, which makes its protection easier and, if there are many additions and suppressions, to effect either periodical re-ordering into heaps so as to make the freed spaces available again (a method called *garbage collecting*) or a chaining of the latter (each creation or addition being made at the head of the chain of blanks).

- By numerical or assimilated calculation if some operations on the pointers lead to the same result. Since we have a free choice of pointers, it is easy to avoid collisions.

- By tackling the translation problem the other way round, by exploring the memory address after address, until retrieving the record sought by its pointers. However, the difficulties met are comparable to those arising for tables and besides the network organization loses its relevance. Thus this access is never used alone, but only for small portions of a network placed in areas designated by their addresses.

- By building up a dictionary of the translations which itself is either a table consisting of pointers and their corresponding addresses or a network having the same function. However, the difficulties encountered are the same as those arising for tables and some of the advantages of the network organization are lost. That is why this access is seldom used alone.

Thus generally speaking, direct translations and translations by calculation are very simple and the only interesting ones if used alone.

Inverted lists

A first compromise consists in using the principle of a dictionary of translations, but fragmented into several lists of addresses. Each pointer, or pointer's fragment, is accompanied by a dictionary of all its possible values, where each of the latter is an entry for all the addresses of the records referred to by such a pointer's value.

Example   A person's name and the national identification number may be fragmented into: the first five consonants of the name (more characteristic than the first five letters), year of birth, month of birth, etc.; a dictionary is made up for consonants, another one for the year, another one for the month, etc. and for each entry, all the addresses of entities where the value of the entry is actualized appear.

The required address is obtained by determining the element common to all the lists of addresses.

Such an organization is called an *inverted list* and permits rapid access if each pointer, or pointer's fragment, has few possible values, otherwise the access in the dictionaries is long (*Figure 5.9*). It is quite suitable – in the case of keys acting as pointers – for logical questions on the keys.

Example   In the preceding example, it is easy to use the lists of addresses in order to answer questions of the type: if born between such and such a date, but not in such or such a month, and so on.

Crossed lists

A second compromise consists in using again the principle of the dictionary of translations, where each pointer – or pointer's fragment – is associated with the dictionary of all its possible values and each of these corresponds to the address at the head of a chain of records referred to by such a value of a pointer.

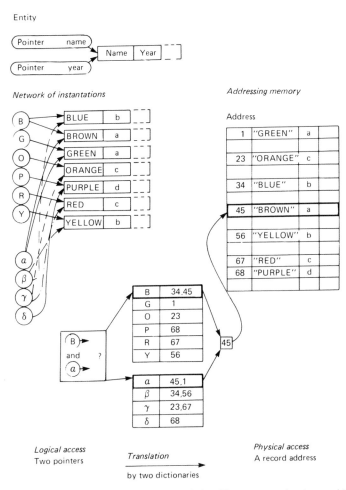

Figure 5.9 Pointer towards address translation. First compromise: inverted list

Example In the preceding file, each dictionary contains the address at the head of a chain whose records have all respectively the same first consonants or the same year of birth, etc.

The required address is retrieved through the simultaneous unrolling of the chains until the element common to all is made out. So each record belongs to as many chains as existing

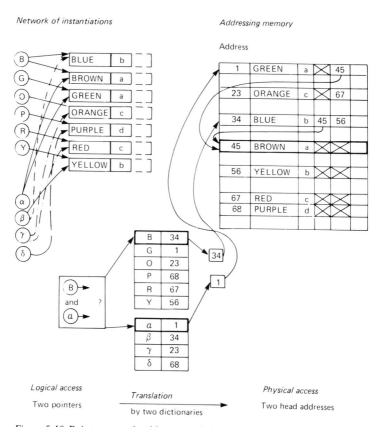

Figure 5.10 Pointer towards address translation. Second compromise: crossed lists

dictionaries. Such an organization, called a *crossed list* (or multilist), permits rapid access when there are few pointers or fragments, otherwise the unravelling of chains takes a long time (*Figure 5.10*). It is quite suitable for simple (not simultaneous) questions when the pointers act as keys.

The two preceding compromises are not simple.

Cell-like organizations

A third compromise consists of combining an access similar to that of the inverted list, but the addresses are those of areas (non-elementary cells of the memory) and, in each area, an access exists similar to that of the cross lists. Such an organization is

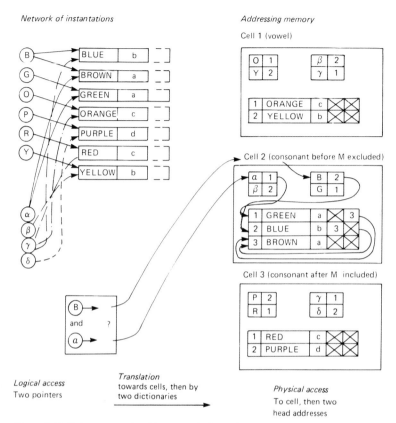

Figure 5.11 Pointer towards address translation. Third compromise: cell-like organization

called *cell-like (Figure 5.11)*. The access is fast when each area corresponds to a distinct memory or at least a fragment easily accessible as a block.

Remark The preceding compromises are organizations with several kinds of pointers. In general they access only one part of the record, the remainder of which is referred to by a new pointer.

Example An organization with several types of pointers may refer to car owners, one pointer sending us back from each of them to the car(s) actually possessed.

Network types

The network structure offers a wide range of types. It is adapted to records which are very closely related to each other and which may be accessed in many different ways (called *access paths*).

Rings

The *ring* (or circular list) is similar to a chain, but the last pointer refers to the head. This organization is adapted to cyclical explorations and avoids the peculiar processing taking place at the end of a chain in algorithms.

Double chains

The *double chain* (or bidirectional list) is organized as a chain in two ways simultaneously: from the head by the 'follower' pointers and from the end by the 'precedent' pointers. This virtually symmetrical organization is adapted to unrollings in two directions. It is convenient for cancellations and also prevents the loss of a pointer from making a chain fragment inaccessible.

Double rings

The *double ring* (or circular bidirectional list) combines the two preceding organizations.

Sequential lines

The *sequential line* (or simple line) is a chain without any record cancellation, where the additions are made only at the end. This organization is not suitable for other updatings, but is adapted to many problems. In most cases the pointers are suppressed except the head one.

Example The set of prime numbers can be determined by building a line with those already discovered and by adding every following number that none of them can divide.

FIFO stacks

The FIFO stack (first in, first out) is a chain where additions are made only at the end and cancellation at the head. It is adapted for many temporary storage problems and keeps the order of creation. Most of the time the pointers are suppressed, except the one at the head, whereas another refers directly to the end. (This amounts to considering that additions are made at the head only and suppressions only at the end).

LIFO stacks

The LIFO stack (last in, first out) is a chain where the additions and suppressions are made only at the head (or what would be equivalent, at the end); the head is then called the top. It is fit for many evaluation problems and most of the time the pointers are suppressed, except the top one.

Remark   As with a chain, the preceding organizations permit only an iterative access, but the algorithms that deal with them are usually recursive, that is, are defined by resorting to their own description.

Example   Determining the pointer in a chain referring to the Nth follower of a record, itself referred to by a pointer P may be done as follows. If P is a nil pointer or if N is null, then it is P; otherwise, do the same search with $N-1$ by replacing P by the follower of the record it refers to.

Example   Determining the pointer in a chain referring to a record of a given value is done in the following manner:

• give P the value of the head pointer;
• if P is a nil pointer or if the value of the referred record is the required one, then it is P;
• otherwise do the same search by replacing P by the follower of the record it refers to.

Binary tree structures

A binary tree structure is called *well ordered* when each node is characterized by a value, and if this value equals at least that of the left descendant, if any, and is lower than that of the right descendant, if any. The retrieval of the pointer referring to one of them is then very simple and efficient. It is solved by the following algorithm:

• give P the value of the root pointer;
• if P is a nil pointer, of if the referred value is the required one, then it is P;
• otherwise

- if the referred value is lower than that required, then search again by replacing the value of P by that of the pointer of the right descendant;
- if the referred value is higher than the required one, then search again by replacing the value of P by that of the pointer of the left descendant.

In a number of problems, we must trace the paths (or walks) of the tree structure, that is, access all these elements in a certain way. The main paths are;

- the prefixed one; we begin with the root, then the left subtree, then the right subtree;
- the postfixed one: we begin with the left subtree, then the right one, then the root;
- the infixed one: we begin with the left subtree, then the root then the right subtree.

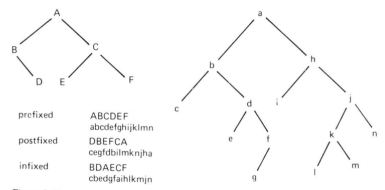

prefixed	ABCDEF
	abcdefghijklmn
postfixed	DBEFCA
	cegfdbilmknjha
infixed	BDAECF
	cbedgfaihlkmjn

Figure 5.12

Remark   All these walks are recursive, the root being given as a calling argument each time:

Prefixed (node)	if node ≠	nil pointer
	then	write (value (node)),
		prefixed (left (node)),
		prefixed (right (node)).
Postfixed (node)	if node ≠	nil pointer
	then	postfixed (left (node)),
		postfixed (right (node)).
		write (value (node)),
Infixed (node)	if node ≠	nil pointer
	then	infixed (left (node)),
		write (value (node)),
		infixed (right (node)).

We may sometimes represent a binary tree without updating in a contiguous way, for instance in a prefixed path with left and right indicators.

Example   The preceding binary tree structure may be depicted as follows:

A g B g d D g d d C g E g d d F g d

Usually however, the display with pointers prevails, either directly deducted from the real layout, or in Ariadne's claw.

The nodes that do not have two descendants are associated with one or two nil pointers. It is convenient to use them in order to point to the follower (the right pointer for instance) and the preceding one (left pointer) in a given path (postfixed or infixed).

In order to suppress any ambiguous meaning of the pointer (true descendant or follower or preceding one in the walk), adding the binary variable of 'true' or 'false' is enough.

To make the display appear symmetrically, the left pointer to the first node in the walk and the right pointer to the last node designate a dummy head node; the left pointer of the latter indicates the root, and the right one, the head node proper.

Example   Ariadne's claw in an infixed path.

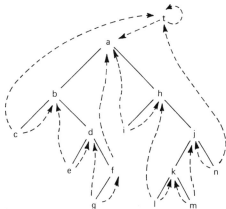

Figure 5.13

Remark   The network data bases are made up from a choice between the preceding organizations.

Items of graphic information are represented by networks; so each top of a polyhedron points to those of a same line and primitives of access supply its sides for instance.

Sorting

Sorting for a table

This consists of sorting out its records in ascending or descending order of the values of a key.

Remark   When we sort a table on two or more keys at the same time, the main order is considered on a key called major and for each of its values, a secondary order, on a key called minor. It makes no difference if the sorting is completed in two stages or simultaneously, since it produces no more problems than sorting on a key.

Sorting for a network

This is done by building a particular path of access, that is a chain, in the ascending or descending order of a characteristic.

Remark   Such a characteristic may be the value of the pointer proper, or that of an element in the record.

So the two cases are not distinct and the only conceptual problem is classifying a set of values, instantiations of the same characteristic entity.

Remark   Of course technical criteria are not fulfilled in the same way when actually sorting records and sorting only pointers. This set of values itself is, intrinsically, a heap devoid of any previous organization.

We may choose to organize it as simply as possible.

- In a vector, because access is fast and there is no creation or cancellation of any record, however, reclassifying is awkward.

Example   When sorting by selection, we proceed through a whole overview so as to find the smallest element, put this one into another vector and then seek the lowest follower (difficulties can arise, though, when some values are equal). When sorting by comparison and transposition, we explore the vector and invert the pairs of successive elements that are out of order until they have all been put in order. When sorting by counting, we determine for each element the number of the lower ones and then put the element in the corresponding place in another vector (difficulties can arise, though, when some values are equal).

• In a sequential file, because there is no need for pointers.

Example A balanced sorting makes up two or more lines from the initial heap by building monotonic series, then it takes them again to lengthen them by building two or more new lines until all the values are classified in a single line.

We may also take into account the results of information theory, which demonstrates that the fastest method simply consists of creating a well-ordered binary tree from the initial heap and then exploring it in the infixed order.

Example Sorting by segmentation divides the heap into two subheaps: one includes only elements that are lower than or equal to an arbitrary value and the other only elements that are higher. Sorting then proceeds in the same way, recursively in each subheap and this method builds a binary tree from the elements and then reorganizes it so that it is in order.

Remark In a sorted vector, the optimal access by value (called dichotomic) consists in seeking in which half the required value is located, and in doing so recursively as well; this is similar to search in a binary tree. That is why the indexes are usually organized in a vector on a well-ordered binary tree.

Conclusion

We have seen that the organizations of entities and their modes of access are numerous and often complex. The main general criterion has been comprehensibility. This means that any choice should be the most natural one, that is, the nearest to that resulting from the relationships between the actual entities in the algorithm. The main technical criterion is the availability of the required organization in the chosen artificial language, since creating its support ourselves is not always easy.

Chapter 6

Structuralism of actions

Introduction

We have seen that an elementary statement is a sentence with a verb, whose structure is:

- to manipulate or describe an entity:

  verb + object + preposition + complement

  or

  verb + indirect object + direct object,

  the preposition usually being one of: in, before, after, while, until, except, between, according to;
- to access an entity:

  interrogative pronoun or adjective or adverb (sometimes a phrase) + clause in the indicative mood,

  the former being usually one of: which, how many, when, how long.

We have seen as well that compound statement is accompanied by an adverbial clause whose structure is:

- to manipulate an entity:

  conjunction of subordination + condition,

  the conjunction possibly being: if, except if, while, until, according to, whether . . . or . . ., when, as long as, whenever, as soon as, after, until the moment when, before;
- to access an entity:

  interrogative pronoun + 'is such as' + condition

  or

  interrogative adverb + entity identifier + 'is such as' + condition.

Lastly we have seen that a collection of statements, those being implicity connected by 'and' can build up a block, or a procedure communicating through parameters and arguments.

Types of actions' structure

We can now simplify the terminology we use by grouping the actions' structures into large categories depending on the prepositions and conjunctions for the manipulation or description statements, and are almost set for the access statements. They depend neither on the verbs (languages are not basically different except in the range of the vocabulary), nor on the entity identifiers (almost freely chosen), nor on the conditions (which may be clearly expressed in semi-mathematical language).

Definitions

Procedures

A procedure is a set of occasionally parametered statements, called to be carried out and supplied with arguments when there are parameters.

Tasks

A task is a procedure carried out simultaneously with one or several other programs.

Blocks

A block is a set of self-sufficient statements.

Sequences

A sequence is a series of statements executed one after the other once and only once invariably. This corresponds, in common language, to statements linked by 'and'.

Remark   Calling a procedure, from the viewpoint of the calling program, is equivalent to executing a sequence.

Logical loops

A logical loop is a series of statements executed successively a certain number of times according to the value of a condition. This corresponds, in common language, to conditional statements using the conjunction 'while', as in:

   while (condition) repeat (sequence),

or the conjunction 'until', as in:

repeat (sequence) until (condition).

These two cases may be expressed by a single structure (which is no longer expressed in common language):

repeat [(sequence); exit if (condition), (sequence)].

The sequence of a logical loop 'while' is not carried out at all if the condition is false from the start. All the forms of logical loops imply that the condition may be evaluated each time, and should end by interrupting the execution of the loop.

Iterative loops

An iterative loop is a series of statements executed successively a precise number of times, for all the elements in a set. This corresponds, in common language, to orders using the prepositions 'in', 'between', as in:

do [(entity) in (set); (sequence)].

Remark   The logical and iterative loops are also called *iteration structures*. These two loops may be combined;

do [(entity) in (set) while (condition) until (condition); (sequence)].

Selections

A selection is several series of statements, one of which at most is executed according to the values of as many conditions as present series. This corresponds in common language to the sentences using the conjunctions 'if', 'except if', 'according to whether . . . or . . .', the adverbs 'else', 'otherwise', or the prepositions 'except', 'according to':

according to whether (condition) (sequence);
            or whether (condition) (sequence);
            or whether (condition) (sequence);
– – – otherwise   (sequence).

Remark   A selection including only one condition is called *conditional*:

if (condition) (sequence).

A selection including only two opposite conditions is called *alternative*:

if (condition) (sequence);
else (condition) (sequence).

Inquiries

An inquiry is an access statement including a descriptive requirement. This corresponds in common language to the varied questions beginning with 'which', 'how many':

which (entity) is such as (requirement)?
how many (entities) are such as (requirement)?

Synchronized sequences

A synchronized sequence is a series of statements carried out once when a time event occurs, or whenever an event occurs, or only until an event occurs. This corresponds, in common language, to orders using the conjunctions 'when', 'just as', 'whenever', 'as soon as', 'after', 'while':

when (event) (sequence);
whenever (event) (sequence);
until the moment when (event) (sequence).

Remark Calling a task is, from the viewpoint of the calling program, equivalent to the beginning of a synchronized sequence execution.

Synchronized loops

A synchronized loop is a series of orders executed indefinitely until an event occurs. This corresponds in common language to statements using the conjunctions 'while', 'whereas', 'as long as', 'at the same time as'.

as long as (non event) (sequence).

Synchronized selections

A synchronized selection is several series of orders, one at most of which is executed according to the occurrence of one event or another. This would correspond in common language to orders using terms of selection and synchronized sequence:

according to whether (event) (sequence);
              or (event) (sequence);
              or (event) (sequence);
– – – otherwise (sequence);

Time queries

A time query is an access order with respect to an event. This corresponds, in common language, to an order using 'when', 'since when' or 'how long':

when (event)?
how long (event)?

Typology

The preceding typology is interesting because it simplifies the development and conveys the generality of algorithms, designs and coding that describe, manipulate and access entities. Besides, it frees us from purely technical and sometimes extremely variable considerations and terminologies.

Thus, most of the time, statements other than queries are intended for the independent translator of the programming language, whereas the queries are designed for the translator of a manipulating language, which is part of the data-base managing system or intended for a separate utility program.

Furthermore, the preceding structures (in some languages which cannot cope with them straightaway) have to be coded using techniques lacking any conceptual interest.

Of course the programmer cannot overlook these points completely, but precise information will be found only in the manufacturers' and service suppliers' manuals since they designed the hardware and software, or result from sheer common sense or from investigative experiments and simulations.

Example Some primitive languages have no selection or any suitable alternative and only permit the execution of a sequence with one condition. This is due to the nature of the electronic circuits and the fact that such languages were created in the early days of programming. This means that the selection and alternative structures have to be translated. In the same way, some languages can take the procedure call only it it is not recursive. That is why, for instance, the recursive process must be translated into a loop (iteration). An even more serious matter is that, when the events cannot be dealt with by a language, the only resource is to partly take up another language.

The preceding typology enables us to separate the conceptual and technical outlooks. It applies to single actions as much as to collections of actions.

Difficulty of choosing actions' structures

The statements that may be expressed in ordinary language are eventually reduced to large categories, each of which is clearly understandable and natural.

The difficulty in choosing the actions' structures in program design thus lies in using these structures simultaneously, that is, to go from the algorithm to a design result combining them. This is not natural and causes a major difficulty in the proceedings where the general rules still play the largest role. As a consequence, the following part of this chapter will be methodical.

Programming using the tree approach

Description

Designing an algorithm described in ordinary language consists of splitting it up into a combination of the structures defined in the preceding typology, namely: procedures, tasks, blocks, sequences, logical loops, iterative loops, selections, inquiries, synchronized sequences, synchronized loops and time queries.

Any designing methodology is limited by:

- the non-unique correspondence between the algorithm and the program, otherwise we might visualize automating the translations of algorithms;
- the impracticability of rigorously proving the accuracy of the design; otherwise we might visualize automating the checking of programs.

Now these two automations are practicable only in very simple and artificial cases. So we cannot expect to carry out a design rigorously but only rationally, so as to best fulfil the general and technical rules.

The whole rational design proceeding springs from the following principle:

To solve the function we must deduce its entities and actions.

In other words, the program design must be carried out from the algorithm by a determination of the information (single or in a collection) and the statements (single or in a collection) needed to solve the required function.

Remark   In order to show straightaway that this principle is not obvious to use, let us consider the design of the following problem. Three existing or imagined words are given, two of four letters and one of five letters. Let us determine all the ways of replacing each letter by a number so that the result of the addition of the two numbers obtained from the first two words is equal to the number obtained from the third word. Different letters cannot have the same value.

Thus, the well-known problem
$$\begin{array}{r} \text{SEND} \\ \underline{\text{MORE}} \\ \text{MONEY} \end{array}$$

is solved in this way:
$$\begin{array}{r} 9567 \\ \underline{1085} \\ 10652 \end{array}$$

This design is difficult. However, carrying it out thoroughly is not necessary, as our aim above all is to check by ourselves that we approach it well and that the proper questions are raised at the right time.

Tree-like design

So the design is tree-like: each piece of information or statement that is too complex to be clearly perceived in a global way (that is be practically written in a simple sentence) and, simultaneously, coded in a very limited number of statements must itself be considered as a function to be solved. Consequently we shall deduce from it the means and actions likely to actualize it and so on. The design will then be appropriately represented by a tree structure or by nested functional blocks (which amounts to the same thing).

Example We are all capable of giving out change when paid more than the due amount. If we wish to program the calculation of coins and banknotes to be given back (for instance to simulate an automatic cash desk before it is built), we may subdivide the function 'give change back' in the following way:

give change back $\begin{cases} \text{calculate amount to be given back,} \\ \text{determine how to give it back.} \end{cases}$

(This is only one way of proceeding. The method often used by traders has been deliberately omitted – they usually add the change to the due amount until they reach the paid amount.) If we use the above breakdown, the calculation of the amount to be given back can be directly coded (except in a primitive language), since it is only a reading followed by a subtraction and the required variables do not need any particular organization. However, determining how to give the change back must be broken up again, so as to give the following tree structures:

give change back
- calculate the amount to be given back
- determine how to give it back
  - calculate the numbers of each type of banknote and coin;
  - print those numbers

(Here again this is only one way of proceeding; there are others, such as calculating each number one by one and printing it at once). If we keep to this solution, we must break down further the calculation of the numbers, but their printing can be coded straight away. Only when we subdivide the calculation of the numbers shall we have to choose the organization of the collection of valid bank notes and coins. Without carrying on with this example, we can see that the design is tree like.

Descendant design

The design is descendant in that the building of the program is naturally descending from the most general function to be achieved until the description of a resource or a treatment may be directly coded. In the designing process, the way the design is represented does not matter as long as the functions remain clear.

It is convenient to use abridged ordinary language and to lay out brackets in the tree (but the dependence relations may just as well be shown in nested blocks).

Example   In a mark-giving program, let us suppose we are given a file of names each followed by a set number of marks, and we want to compute the total score for each name.

The function to be shown (compute the total mark for each name) requires an input file and a vector of coefficients as entities; the action is the calculation of a total mark for each. At the first stage, the design is then:
- define an input file
- define and initialize a vector of coefficients
- until the end of the file: compute and print the global mark for the current name

The definition of the file is often implicit and need not be coded (but may be mentioned in a comment), that of the vector and its initialization can be directly coded (except when a low-level language is used), as well as the formulation of a loop ending with the end of the file.

The remainder deserves further analysis. Computing the total mark for a particular name requires the resources of an output file, an area to read and write the name as well as a vector in order to place the detailed marks, and as action the calculation of the two vectors' dot product (one of coefficients, the other of partial marks) followed by the printing. This second stage in the design is then:

$$
\text{compute and print the total mark for the current name}
\begin{cases}
\text{define}
\begin{cases}
\text{an output file} \\
\text{an area for the name} \\
\text{a vector for the partial marks}
\end{cases} \\[2ex]
\text{read name and vector of partial marks} \\
\text{compute dot product: coefficients} \\
\text{multiplied by partial marks} \\[1ex]
\text{print it with the name}
\end{cases}
$$

Everything can be directly coded, except, possibly, the dot product.

This design opposes the two following procedures:

- computing the dot product, putting a loop around it, and lastly writing the management statements (area reservation, etc.);
- writing the management statements, where these would have been written first.

Continuous design

The design is then said to be *continuous*, until we may let the language directly express the required resource or action. It remains independent of the language (at least in so far as the latter does not exclude wording a request for resource or for an action), but is stops relatively early according to the power of the language in question. For instance extracting a chain fragment, inverting a matrix, sorting a series of numbers are all commonplace occurrences in some languages but not in all.

Example   In the preceding problem, if we use a language that enables us to express the dot product without a loop, the last stage of the design is not needed. If, on the other hand, the condition of an empty file cannot be expressed directly in the language used in the loop or in the reading order, then a last special card test has to be set up. This variant is, however, of little importance as it needs to be taken into account only when the design reaches the end.

Stepwise refinement

It can be seen that the above design proceeds through a stepwise refinement of the entities and actions. In particular, at each stage, only the characteristics that prove necessary for the entities are imposed. In this way unnecessary precautions are avoided (for example, using an array where a scalar number is sufficient, or vector fit for one stack, and so on). At least they are explicit in the case when the language forces us to use an ill-adapted type of data structure.

Remark   As the variables appear in the design at the location where they are first used, we are not so prone to make the frequent mistake of forgetting their (re-)initialization (particularly of counters and arrays). The incompatibility of the characteristics between the calling arguments and the parameters of a procedure is also more obvious; besides, the array of cross references between the entities' names and the line of the statement (when the compiler supplies it) is much more useful.

Another consequence is that only calls limited to the range of a well-defined function need to be solved, and the programmer's intentions are more clearly made out than in the maze inherent with the use of jumps. Furthermore the mistakes and awkward moves often caused by jumps (such as the omission of a branch or an artificially isolated case) are then reduced or suppressed.

Functional modularization

We can now see that the design proceeds through functional modularization. In particular, each module that actualizes a well-defined function has a characterized validity range and may be mechanically (except for practical reasons) performed by a sequence or the call of a procedure or a task.

Remark   The advantage of widely using procedures and tasks lies not only in avoiding repetition of the same sequences, but also in enabling us to single out their function more clearly.

Another consequence is the clarity of intent as they build up a whole with well-defined inputs and outputs. Ideally a routine should have only one input and one output.

Advantages and restraints

The characteristics of a rational procedure are thus established: the design should be a tree structure (which may be descendant where appropriate) continuous, go through stepwise refinement and functional modularization. This method is infinitely better than an empirical approach or a collection of dodges, tricks or maxims. However, we cannot endow our methodology with absolute value, as we can see if we look at a case where it is not observed.

Remark   There is a frequent contradiction between the partial and often insecure advantages of dodges and the overall interest inherent in the rules, and that is one of craftmanship versus industry. Experience shows also that most mistakes are caused by bending the rules and not misinterpreting the dodges.

We must avoid thinking that the preceding methodology makes any design simple, or that determining the necessary functions is always obvious. In particular, it is not possible to prescribe the building of a complete design branch by branch or level after level. This is all a matter of common sense or preference but, going back over earlier steps is practically unavoidable when the algorithm is a complex one. On the other hand, when it is simple, there is no use in resorting to this methodology to help intuition; what matters above all is ability and training.

It is also possible that some good reason may lead us not to follow these rules. First, the structure of the entities may be imposed upon us from outside and then the design cannot logically be deduced from the functions to be solved; besides, some entities may happen to be shared and their very existence is previously determined.

Another point is that the structure of the actions may be mostly a set of complex sequences and procedures with loose and entangled relations: it then proves more efficient and natural to design the sequences and procedures separately, then to combine them in an ascending way.

Lastly, the processing of the tasks gives rise to problems that will be tackled later and are not all solved by a structured design for each of them.

Remark   Artificial languages sometimes prompt us to make partly empirical choices in cases when logical decisions would be difficult, all the more so when the languages are primitive. For example, some jumps (by themselves totally irrational) are convenient and cannot be criticized if they do not destroy the inherent structure of the program. The most serious drawback is when some languages cannot express the inclusion of a procedure or a block into another procedure or block. The design then has to be artificially fragmented just like a book that could not be written in chapters, paragraphs and subparagraphs but only in subparagraphs put one after the other randomly and coherence achieved by hopping from one to the other. Thus we can consider the preceding methodology as a rational but not universally applicable procedure and shall now examine it with respect to compliance with the general rules of program design.

Observance of the rules of program design

Feasibility rule

Designing in a tree structure interferes little with the observance of the feasibility rule. Yet as such a design proceeds at once through an attempt at splitting up functions expressed in natural language, an ambiguous or ill-defined problem must appear as such much earlier. We therefore have to think before launching into the design.

Example   Suppose we have to find the words that actually exist that may be built from a phone number with three letters corresponding to each digit appearing in the phone number. Even if we give (which is of no help) the number of digits in the numbers and the existing words, the problem is ambiguous and its purpose not clear enough.
The design will effectively have to be carried out in many different ways depending on whether the program must define the words to be built from one single given number – in which case it will consist of a retrieval and a mere suppression in the dictionary whose structure will be a line – or whether the program must determine those words for any single number. In that case we shall have to build the dictionary in a tree structure so that its sweeping is not prohibitive, or even build up, once and for all, a dictionary of the numbers corresponding to the existing words so that we can search first for the given number in it, then for the words to which it corresponds.

Versatility and generality rules

Since the function of a program is likely to change to some extent, the description of entities and actions must be easily adaptable and alterable, otherwise, it is better to keep an unadapted description. Besides, we do not always know exactly what we want and the best way to get it before we have run the program and tried some variants.

Of course no procedure can guarantee that the utility domain of a program will be alterable or expandable at minor cost. But as designing in a tree structure splits it up into functions, it proves easier both to locate the changes to be done and make them. Any alteration of a function is effectively limited to one level in the tree, and unless we change the problem all the rest of the design remains valid and does not require re-examining. Furthermore it then becomes possible to check the programs of closely related functions separately in order to choose the preferred version.

Example   If we look again at the problem of giving back change, we can see that whenever the currency changes – by particular denomination being cancelled or created – the program will have to be re-written if the number of banknotes and coins, the size of the vector of the values, its components and the ends of the iterative loops have not been left variable. Depending on the way we calculate each number, the consequences of choosing other units of change may be more or less important. For instance, instead of giving back the change with the highest value (as we take it for granted that the stock is well supplied with such change), we may prefer to get rid of the most numerous values in stock. When a program is properly designed, it may have a vast validity domain, and so be used again without any notable alteration for unexpected cases. Thus the preceding program might consist of a given mass from a set of weights, and even display the numbers according to certain codes.

Remark   Some simple devices for improving versatility do exist, but in small number, as versatility lies mainly in a proper design of the functions.

A tree structure naturally prompts us to retain independence of particular data since we proceed by keeping our design general as long as possible especially when the amount of data transferred to each module remains low. Besides, we should make intensive use of parameterized modules and not insert any hindrance to the general character of the design. For example, the inappropriate constant limit of a loop is a uselessly restricted format. In the same way it is often better to use an initialized variable rather than a constant. There is no need to get the greatest possible versatility at any cost, but versatility proves more often to be insufficient than excessive.

Rules of functional modularization and planning

The main role of functional modularization is to ensure the adaptation of entities and actions, their consistency and homogeneity.

Wondering whether the means and actions are well adapted (in particular whether they are better adapted than others) makes sense only if we have a precise knowledge of the function involved. The validity domain of any independent module has then to be perfectly well defined and present itself as the design is in progress. This elementary consideration, when properly applied, enables us to cancel meaningless procedures and occasionally avoids unpleasant surprises, such as the use of routines whose validity domain is more restricted than that of the calling program, processing going on in spite of a loss of numerical meaning, tests on absolute magnitude, unexpected cases and so on. Of course, no processing is valid when the means required have not been obtained, in particular when the elements have not previously been well defined and assigned (initialized for variables).

This requirement is obvious, but no procedure can ensure that the means and actions are adapted, let alone that they are optimal. Nevertheless, design in a tree structure leads to a program split up into functions. At least we know what each part (level in the tree) is supposed to do, that is, we know the meaning of each resource required and also that each action performed is clear and that their validity range results from it.

Example In the design of the problem of giving change, we can see the second stage of the tree structure: 'determine how to give it back' is when we have to choose a data structure in order to represent the number of banknotes and coins. We can choose either a scalar variable by kind, or a vector, or a stack if the number of different kinds cannot be considered as already known. Similarly, only when we split up the third level: 'compute the number of each banknote and coin' shall we have to choose the representation of the values of banknotes and coins, and the latter will be more easily adapted than if it had been chosen from the very beginning.

Moreover, the validity range of the second level 'determine how to give it back' (positive or null amount) is made more clearly explicit by an independent calculation of the amount.

A consequence of the functional modularization is to facilitate planning as each independent function may be actualized then tested separately in its lapse of actualization. Integration, that is the combining of different modules, is simplified, as each functional module is adapted to a whole, as the element of a globally conceived entirety. Another consequence is to enable the only genuine optimization, namely a global one.

Optimization, the research for improving means and actions, makes sense only if the means and actions are first well adapted to the problem. Before trying to discover 'tricks of the trade' in detail, we must set up the basic principle of the solution. No general method can enable us to find one, but design in a tree structure may help us indirectly because it forces us to think before we start and define the functions clearly. We have to think in a correct, rather than narrow, way.

Example   It would be useless to optimize a program meant to generate all the prime numbers below a given limit, if the aim would be to know whether a given number were prime or not. It would be equally useless to generate a program adapted to the sorting of numbers slightly out of order and use it to sort out badly disorganized records or even to compute a sum of decreasing terms with many significant digits for a very accurate result when only a rough value is necessary.

It is only when we have found the correct general principle needed to solve the problem that it makes sense to deal with the details and try to improve the solution. Should it prove wrong, it is just as well to realize it as early as possible, even if only by trying it manually and doing it all over again from the beginning.

Keeping our purpose in mind also helps us to know whether we should optimize (is there any need if the program is run only once or if the optimization is more expensive?) and, in that case, where we should optimize. Efforts should bear on the critical modules (if not the most time consuming, at least the most expensive) and not the least elaborate ones. These critical modules are partly revealed by design in a tree structure, and where we cannot evaluate beforehand, the resulting structure at least enables us to insert counters that give us an idea of the different running times, unless the software directly provides the numbers of executions of each statement or the global time lags spent on each instruction. Moreover, the techniques of software and hardware (pagination of the virtual memories) allow programs to be split up into modules. In addition, before hoping to get an efficient program straight-away, we shall already have a working program.

Example   Here is the design of a program printing the calendar of any month in the twentieth century.

Determining each day amounts to calculating (modulo 7) the number of days elapsed since 1 January 1901 which fell on a Monday. This calculation may be divided into three elements:

● number of days elapsed in the century until the first of January in the year considered ('coefficient of the year'). As 365 equals modulo 7, it is the number of the year plus the whole part of the quotient of that number divided by 4 (leap years).

● number of days elapsed in the year until the first day of the month considered, taking into account a possible 29th of February (coefficient of the month).

● number of days elapsed since the beginning of the month (day of the month).

These calculations might be summed up in a very limited number of lines and even in a single line depending on the language used. But it is better to keep them individual for each module, and so to proceed by breaking up a version that is already correct, but not yet optimized.

calculate – print
the calendar
{

define and initialize the vectors of the
names of days and months
define and initialize the vector of the
numbers of days and months

read month and year

(for each day
of the month)
determine the name $\left\{\begin{array}{l}\text{calculate its}\\\text{number}\\\text{take its name}\end{array}\right.$
of the day
print it with its number in the month

$$
\text{calculate the number of the day}
\begin{cases}
\begin{array}{l}
\text{(function)} \\
\text{return} \quad \text{(coefficient of the year} \\
\qquad\qquad + \text{ coefficient of the month} \\
\qquad\qquad + \text{ day of the month)}
\end{array} \\[2em]
\begin{array}{l}
\text{coefficient} \\
\text{of the year}
\end{array}
\begin{cases}
\text{(function)} \\
\text{return (year} + \text{integer} \\
\quad \text{part(year/4)}
\end{cases} \\[2em]
\begin{array}{l}
\text{coefficient} \\
\text{of the month}
\end{array}
\begin{cases}
\text{(function)} \\
\text{return (sum of the} \\
\quad \text{days of the months} \\
\quad \text{elapsed} + 1 \text{ if and} \\
\quad \text{only if the year} \\
\quad \text{is a leap year, and} \\
\quad \text{February elapsed)}
\end{cases}
\end{cases}
$$

This design of the calendar problem is certainly not optimal from the point of view of running time. For each day of the month the number of the day is determined, whereas calculating the first day of the month and then iterating it on the follower, would suffice, and each time we recalculate the sum of the numbers of days of the months elapsed before.

This does not mean that the design is bad (except if it was the latest version of a much used program). Most of the rules, however, are observed, in particular the practicability of testing and understanding the program (and 'improving' it for a limited number of uses at the risk of spending some more checking time would not be economic).

Remark Simple devices for improving adaptation do exist, but considerations of global optimization (including the work of the program designer) must not be taken as promptings to laziness (except to a form of intelligent laziness); such considerations only apparently contradict the underlying concerns about saving running time and memory space which are taught to all beginners learning a language.

The common blunders are trivial, so are the methods of avoiding them: to do without conversions, not to read what can be computed, not to assign instead of initializing, to avoid indices and numerous entangled loops, etc., or they spring from common sense (not to redetermine a date printed several times, but keep it in an area, etc). Some refinements must be used carefully, so a transfer by argument and parameter certainly costs more than by outside elements stored in a common area. However, such transfers make procedures interact inconspiciously, which can be the source of many errors.

Many tricks require in-depth knowledge of the machine and compiler; consequently they are justified only for exceptionally intensive use (such as for the core of several entangled loops in a current program) and when the compiler can not perform the same way cheaper. Besides, transfer on to another machine may have the opposite effect. However, most of the time it is cheaper to entangle loops (loops with numerous steps inside) in order to re-initialize them as rarely as possible, to deal with arrays in the order of their locations in the memory, to recalculate constant and simple expressions rather than store them (immediate addressing), to set up a chain of tests so that only the rare cases have to follow all the links, to raise to an integer power, preferably to a real power or to a repetitive multiplication and so on.

The procedure must always be to set up a proper design, then possibly to seek optimization without questioning the design.

Reliability and testing strategy rules

In testing that the result of the design genuinely solves the required function, we come across two obstacles:

- no method enables us to assert, in general cases, that a program is correct;
- attempts, however numerous and well-chosen they may be, can be presumed to be correct only as long as they do not encompass all the possible cases exhaustively (which is generally quite impracticable).

So we are compelled to check and adapt our designs by trial and error without being able to expect a guarantee that they will work. Fortunately a design carried out in a tree structure can be checked methodically. As the principle of the tree-structure method is to think about functions, testing must determine whether each function is solved. Wanting to check validity makes sense because it is clearly defined (knowing what we want to check being important when we want to avoid redundant or, on the reverse, incomplete tests, or more random tracings and impressions). Every level can be tested separately as it has a function and an accurate validity domain.

Example   The calculation of a square root for a real number, or of wages, must print a diagnosis of error at once when there is a negative quantity to deal with.

This requires the tests must check (by sample taking) the working of each module unit over its whole validity range and within its limits; a concern for reliability must prompt us to integrate and even incorporate, after adapting, programmed tests warranting that whatever work is required in each module actually belongs to its domain, in particular for data read.

Example   In the design of the change-giving problem, we have to test, between the two parts of the first level (computing the amount to be given back and determining how to give it back) whether the amount is positive or null, for if it is null, the second part cannot be performed (it would supply a result which could only be meaningless).

Similarly, if the first part of the second level (compute the number of each banknote and coin) is divided this way then we have:

$$
\text{compute the number of each banknote and coin}
\left\{
\begin{array}{l}
\left\{
\begin{array}{l}
\text{get and store the number of valid} \\
\quad \text{banknotes and coins} \\
\text{get and store the value of each in an} \\
\quad \text{increasing order} \\
\text{initalize a variable 'remaining amount' to} \\
\quad \text{'amount'}
\end{array}
\right. \\
\left\{
\begin{array}{l}
\left\{
\begin{array}{l}
\text{(for each value as long as} \\
\quad \text{'remaining amount' is non-null)}
\end{array}
\right. \\
\text{calculate and store the} \\
\quad \text{corresponding number} \\
\text{calculate the new 'remaining} \\
\quad \text{amount'}
\end{array}
\right.
\end{array}
\right.
$$

We suppose, implicitly, that the stocks for each banknote and coin are unlimited.

The function has to be solved even in limit cases; for instance, a null account to be given back.

The testing strategy should proceed like the design itself, namely in a tree-like way (that is descending, continuous, by stepwise refinement) and dealing with functional modules.

Testing is descending. The earlier a mistake is discovered, the less it costs; yet the conception may be wrong from the start because of an ill-defined problem, or a mistake in the algorithm. So the design of any important problem (say, providing a program of over a page) must be tested from the beginning.

Any modules not yet written can be reduced to a print enabling us to check they have been called, or to return precalculated results.

All the practicable ways should be checked, which would not be feasible for a program of any length without a tree-structured design. The structure avoids too many points of input and output as well as branchings (especially backwards).

Checking is continuous and proceeds by stepwise refinement, each actualization of a function having first to test that what it receives is in the validity range of its own processing. Here again the sooner a mistake has been detected, the cheaper it is to correct it.

Remark   Print what is read systematically: innumerable mistakes are sought in the processing whereas their cause is the reading format, or one piece of added or missing data. If possible, check how reasonable the data seems and try retrieval in case of error, or at least a diagnosis while testing. It is also wise to check the consistency of outputs (placing of a root in an equation, etc.) without overdoing the number of checking prints, which would dissuade people from reading them carefully.

It is useful to test not only normal checking data sets (if possible, the result of which has been predetermined) but also the limit cases and exceptions, which both reveal omissions in design and checking (in particular divisions by zero and over-filled arrays).

Example   A program for solving quadratic equations will have to be tested on specific cases (each of the coefficients being null, then two, then the three of them, a double root, no real solution) before being used; a program for mixing sorted files will have to foresee the repetition of records, disorder, the presence of an aberrant record, the lack of a necessary one, etc.

A limit case which is particularly useful to test, when possible, is that when a program hardly does anything at all, for example, dimensioning an array to turn it into a scalar or lowering a limit to its inferior value. This may reveal in particular a lot of defects in the loops (wrongly initialized or ended).

We must test a module throughly before inserting it, because the localization of an error will obviously be simplified, all the more so if the module is short.

To be thorough, this method of progressive checking requires only a number of tests proportional to the length of the program, whereas it increases rapidly whenever a complication is added, if there is no tree-structure design.

Example   In the problem of printing an amount in letters as we
have studied before, checking should logically be carried out as
follows. First, the whole program is tested with a dummy
module unit of transcription of the three digits (sending back
only a diagnosis showing it has effectively been called, or simply
that the three digits that were fed into 'it'; the validity domain of
the whole being, for instance, numbers from 0 to 9 999, 999, or
99. We must test that the program deals correctly with these
limits, refuses numbers (negative ones in particular) not
included between them, and works properly for a few numbers
of different size ranges and peculiar cases of insertion, such as
one million, one thousand, one, one million and one dollar or
pounds, one million and one cent or penny.

We can test the module of transcription of three digits with a
dummy calling program. It is conceivable to run it from 0 to 999,
but a test on the numbers from 0 to 100 and a few others might
be considered as enough. Lastly we check the whole.

Remark   Some easy tricks to improve reliability do exist. Within
the limited frame of our discussion so far, some of them enable
us to increase the reliability of the programs, by setting up a list
of our mistakes (because we are often prone to fall into the same
trap several times) and distrusting compilers which cannot
detect all the syntactical mistakes because they themselves must
be optimized for practical purposes. When a compiler especially
designed for checking such mistakes is available, use it first. For
each error, re-test the whole and try not to keep to your first
possible reasons; isolate the testing lines by comments, then
eventually turn them into comments rather than discarding
them. Lastly, do not persist in correcting a program which will
not work but find someone to explain it to, or start it all over
again. However, this is not likely to occur if the design and its
checking have really followed the tree-structure, except when a
syntactical characteristic has remained unknown.

Comprehensibility and security rules

As the function of a program is not only to run on a machine but
also (with certain exceptions) to remain comprehensible by man
and communicable (even if only for a later adaptation), the
required resources and processings should be clearly shown and
well documented.

Whatever the language used may be, we cannot usually expect
to be able to read and assimilate a program quickly. However, the

task is made simpler when the intentions and the procedures followed are emphasized.

This double emphasis is a natural consequence of tree-structured design. As a matter of course, it enables:

- emphasis on the intentions: the tree structure makes the reader understand the roles of entities and actions because the intentions that lead to its development appear in the tree itself and show the meaning of what is designed, then coded.

  Giving examples of programs that are harder to understand than their very functions would no doubt be useless; happy is the man or woman who has never had to trace an organigram from a program and from there try to guess its purpose.

- emphasis on the running: the running of a program (written exactly in the way it was designed, in a tree structure) follows the visual and intellectual representation (vizualizing an iterative or recursive execution usually arouses no difficulty). There are two drawbacks, however: in the selection of cases, some parts of the program are not run, and any use of asynchronism (simultaneous runs or runs triggered by occurrences of events) is impossible to express in a natural and permanent way in the text of a program, since it refers to time. A given formalism of the actual representation might be convenient, especially when several people work on the same design, but this is a minor point.

We may notice in passing that the highest levels of a tree structure design are, most of the time, understandable by non-programmers. This comprehensibility is a main factor of security.

Remark   A lot of easy tricks to improve comprehensibility do exist: they enable articulateness in the preceding frame of the tree structure. The optimization of the program often prevents it from being clear, so in order to use it in the best way, we must be aware not only of running time but also of people's time, and realize that extra testing due to a so-called optimization is often unrewarding.

So here are the main tricks we should keep in mind:

- If a choice has to be made, prefer an articulate wording to a condensed or artful one. Most of the time we underestimate the number of times people will have to understand the program and maintain it and that we usually overrate out memories.

Example We must let the detail of what we do be apparent. Avoid long lines (no more than a dozen variables or constants); complex, particularly logical, expressions; constants whose value is mysterious (of the kind of $\pi/180$, already computed); and too many intermediary variables (especially on an optimizing compiler).

Expressly our meaning as straightforwardly as possible by avoiding entangled processings and, if need be, by putting an empty order to make an empty case explicit. Code uniformly in the same program when several methods are available, for instance, use standard formats, classify the declarations at the head of each module unit in an unvarying order, and so on. As we have already mentioned, these rules for good codings may contradict the reflexes a beginner might acquire. For example, it is bad to encourage a beginner to multiply variables or parentheses, but it would be just as bad in a business program, (especially with a powerful machine and a sophisticated compiler) to use the same variable a hundred times with different meanings, or to go so far to avoid parentheses that a phrase stops being understood at once by a good programmer.

- Use the same rule of clarity in style especially when more or less primitive language is used. Avoid phoney gimmicks which are given as tricks of the trade, and a falsely subtle approach which hides inefficiency.
- Take special care of the physical layout: variable margins, blank lines for paragraphing, good use of blanks (especially between data), to emphasize the structure of the program and particularly the loops and branches of selections, legible prints and named results. In the case where a function must be solved by a large number of statements, it may prove more advantageous for the sake of legibility to make an independent module unit of it.
- Use significant and unambiguous names whenever possible. If abbreviating them is necessary, then keep the initial letters and preferably beginning and consonants.
- Make proper use of the comments, especially at the beginning of the program, they are useful for references. Give the list of the necessary resources, as well as an evaluation of the memory space and the computing time. In the program, comments enlighten the meaning of the statements, provided they explain intentions and are not only

descriptive. A person who would need comments like 'reading' or 'test' would have few chances of understanding the program. On the other hand, it is highly recommended that the sentences and words written during the tree-structure design are turned into comments.

But too many comments soon make a program unreadable; the best documentation is a proper structure according to functions, which can be provided only by a correct design.

Lastly, flow charts, showing the actions as intricate lines, do not explain much and take a long time to draw and alter. They should be reserved at most for training beginners and representing very small modules or, on the reverse, the general lines of a program.

Parallel executions

Task and event

As we have seen, a task is a procedure run parallel with others and the occurrence of an event is comparable to the change of value of a logical variable. This change may result from the passing of time, from a sensor, or the execution of another task.

Sequence loops and selection synchronization; time queries

We have also seen that a design can be expressed in sequence loop and selection synchronized by an event, and we can access the time entity by a time query.

Synchronization itself does not produce any methodological design problem or technical difficulty. As long as there is no interference between tasks we can consider conceptually that they are developed successively and the sensors allow us to take time and the occurrence of events into account.

Priorities

Practically, we must determine priorities for the execution of competing (but not interfering) tasks according to running time and in particular external consideration. For example, two tasks may need the same processor or sensor or the same way of communication simultaneously and cannot share this entity. The priority task then acts upon the other directly to put it off temporarily, then to dispose of the entity and later to take it up (such put-offs and take-ups are only particular synchronized sequences) or it is a third task which settles the conflict.

Example   In a processor, there usually is a utility program (real-time operating system) which plays the role of an arbitrator.

Remark   The processing of a mistake at the execution time can be assimilated by the occurrence of an event triggering the execution of a synchronized sequence, when the take-up does not always occur (fatal error).

The effector and inconsistent states

The only, but considerable, difficulty arouses when several tasks need the same effector or sensor–effector, in particular the same memory.

Effectively the intervention of several tasks on the same effector, not necessarily simultaneously, may lead to inconsistent states which may not be reproduced, or to the suppression of an expected effect.

Example   In an air-ticket booking system, a first task (terminal) can read that a seat is free, then a second task (anchor terminal) could read the same thing. If no precaution has been taken, each of the tasks could accept a reservation without taking into account that only the result is inconsistent. In the same way, in the manipulation of a tool, a first task can make it move, then a second takes it back to its first position. Lastly, the first one makes it work: the result of the move is null.

In that case we no longer master the passing of entities from a consistent state to another.

Transactions

A sequence of actions taking an entity from one coherent state to another is known as a transaction. The same difficulty arises when a task successively accesses several logical related entities which may be altered during access time.

Example   When a task accesses a file of the planned flights then another file of the enrolled passengers, a flight and the reservations may be cancelled just after the first access but before the second one, through another task. Here again the result is inconsistent.

Critical phase and mutual exclusion

The lapse of time when a sequence of actions on an entity is indivisible is known as the *critical phase*. The sequence of actions cannot be interrupted nor can another action be carried out on the same entity without itself running the risk of leading to a null or inconsistent state.

This difficulty arises whether the entity is to be allocated, (temporarily assigned to a task) or disposable (destroyed after assignment).

Example   A telecommunication line is an entity to be allocated, a message is a disposable entity.

During a critical phase proper to an entity, any two tasks likely to access it are said to be in mutual exclusion.

Example   Two tasks, one of which delivers messages in a memory area and the other one of which retrieves them to print them, are in mutual exclusion, the critical phase being the lapse of time when the area is being filled and is then not in a consistent state. Moreover, when any message has to be printed, a synchronization should forbid its replacement by another one as long as it has not been printed.

Remark   This problem of consistency is particularly acute when the entities are very numerous and scattered, especially in the data bases overlapping several distinct locations.

Competition, locks and semaphore

When the tasks are not in real competition, that is, when they are not subfunctions of the same function, the entity can be protected during the critical section to block any other task which is in mutual exclusion and which tries to access it. The protection is called a lock. The entity is locked at the beginning of the critical phase and a third task suspends any task trying to access it. The entity is then unlocked at the end of the critical phase and the third task puts back into action, one by one, all the tasks having attempted access (in an order possibly imposed by the priorities).

Remark   Many practical problems arise because of:

- the need for the lock to be effected instantly (before another task may require it for itself);

- the choice of the precise entity to be locked (a whole file, a record, a fragment of a record);
- the nature of the lock;
- the consequences of a mistake which entails the end of the execution of the task before it has been unlocked (or the omission of that action);
- the possible occurrence of a previous reservation.

The third task mentioned above is often singled out (utility part of the operating system) in a processor. When missing, or if the management of priorities is defective, a task may be blocked indefinitely.

A lock may restrict to a given number of tasks (more than two) the access to a shared entity, not subject to mutual exclusion, but which cannot either be accessed simultaneously by any number of tasks. Such a lock is known as a *semaphore*.

Example A communication line can transmit only a limited number of messages simultaneously.

Cooperation, guards and messages

When tasks are in cooperation, that is when they are subfunctions of the same function, and happen to be in competition, they may be connected by events and use synchronized sequences, loops or selections so as to avoid coming together at a critical phase (or too many of them attempting access to a shared entity).

Remark Each sequence of a synchronized selection is said to be protected by a guard and the tasks able to be blocked that way have a rendezvous.

These events are often called messages as all the entities other than the tasks can transmit to one another, and of which they are particular cases.

Remark Many practical problems arise from the mutual knowledge of the names of the blocking task and of the blocked task, and by the fact that the message itself is an entity in mutual exclusion.

Simultaneous executions cause two basic difficulties for the program designer:

- it is hard for us to conceive simultaneous running, because our minds can only grasp one execution at a time;
- it often is impracticable to test, even by experiment, all the possible cases that might come up, especially if the tasks are in real competition and not in cooperation.

Deadlocks

Another practical difficulty is the deadlock. It occurs when a first task blocks a second one about any entity, then requires another entity, which is itself blocked by the second task itself waiting to be unblocked, to set it free; or when there is a similar delay between several tasks. The solution may be:

- prevention: a third task reserving all the accessed entities before execution, provided we know them in advance, which is not always possible;
- avoidance: a third task allowing each locking of entity only if no risk of deadlock can occur by it; this is very complex and awkward;
- detection and cure: a third task coming up in order to undo all that a task had performed since the cause of deadlock (cancellation of a transaction), to suspend it and later put it back into action, provided that a trace of the transactions is kept;
- the timestamp of the transactions with the suppression of the locks: a third task having to deal with the actual accesses in the chronological order of the stamps.

Remark   The problems which software engineering has to solve in distributed information processing systems are not conceptually different from those caused by the parallel execution of tasks sharing entities (including the lines of communication). These are often managed by specific utility programs.

Index